WHAT'S BEHIND THE WORDS?

RON LEMCO

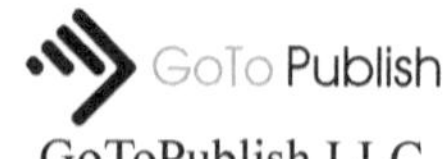

GoToPublish LLC
1-888-337-1724
www.gotopublish.com
info@gotopublish.com

Contents

Introduction v
Chapter 1...1
Chapter 2 6
Chapter 3 12
Chapter 4 16
Chapter 5 20
Chapter 6 25
Chapter 7 31
Chapter 8 35
Chapter 9 38
Chapter 10.. 42
Chapter 11 90
Chapter 12 93
Chapter 13..95
Chapter 14..98
Chapter 15..101
Chapter 16..103
Chapter 17..105
Chapter 18..107
Chapter 19..109
Chapter 20 113
Chapter 21..116
Chapter 22 119
Chapter 23 123
Chapter 24 125
Chapter 25 128

Chapter 26 132
Chapter 27 135
Chapter 28 138
Chapter 29 141
Chapter 30 144
Chapter 31...147
Chapter 32 150
Chapter 33 154
Chapter 34 161
Chapter 35 164
Chapter 36 167
Chapter 37 171
Chapter 38 173
Chapter 39 175
Chapter 40 180
Chapter 41...183
Chapter 42 188
Chapter 43 192

INTRODUCTION

I always thought I was a poet! I have written between 500 and 600 poems over my lifetime…and now I have come to the realization that I am not a poet; I am a rhymer. I want to be like "Dr. Seuss".

The problem I have with poetry, true poetry, is in truly understanding it. I take in the colorful words and the intense yet delightful descriptions, but it never fills me with the meaning of the message the poet was trying to convey.

Maybe I'm an idiot and lack the moxie and the intellect, or maybe it's that I am easily bored. If the reading doesn't grab me right off, I quit reading. Well, who am I to judge? What do I know? What could I have to tell? What is my story?

Before we get to me, I have words to give to you. Here is where I preach to you about the power of keeping a journal. If you take nothing else from this book beyond seeing the power of keeping a journal, then I am as happy knowing you will benefit. It's something you will never regret. Whether you've ever thought of keeping one or not, now is the time to start. Write a paragraph every few days. It becomes easier, and almost a must-do to make your day complete as it becomes a habit.

I, like most people, believe I have led an interesting life. What sets me apart from 95% of our population is the fact that I have recorded my life in journals. I can relive my life anytime I pick up one of the 30 journals I have. We all find ourselves in situations that we have been in before. Through my journals, I can find out how I handled them and if it worked. I know what to do, and if nothing else, I know to try something different. But the biggest advantage for keeping a journal is that when something is bothering me, I write it in my journal. And when I do, I let it go;

I let the journal worry about it. If something is bothering me and there is nothing, I can do about it at that moment... why worry? I have written it down. I can go back to it on my own terms and try to analyze it later. Many times, it wasn't a problem after all, and it fixed itself. Worrying played no part in the problem getting fixed.

We all have had some great times in our lives, and some of us have taken photos of these moments. Now add to your experience, with your words about that day, by journaling about it on the same day that you had all that enjoyment. It will enhance that moment in time, and anytime you want, you can relive those great experiences. On a bad day, a journal becomes a haven of good thoughts and is a vessel for your troubled mind to drift away on.

What is my book about? "What's Behind the Words" is a collection of some funny short stories. They Are stories that are seen through my eyes. It is a compilation of my poems throughout past years combined with the feelings that inspired those poems. Hopefully, by conveying where my head was at the time of the writing, it will give the reader a better understanding of each poem.

I have my journal as a reference. These short stories are not poems; however, in my mind, they reflect poetry.

I want to thank the following people, without whom there would never have been "What's Behind the Words?"

Barbra Burnsed
For having faith in me and a fantastic help in editing.

Freddie Burnsted
For providing me funding, no questions asked.

Drew Lemco
My Teacher son with an English degree, who kept me inspired and helped in editing and cover design.

Destiny Lemco
My Daughter who not only helped edit, but did the format and found the photos inserted.

Valarie Lemco
My Wife, for keeping me going and being my best friend again.

God
For allowing me to be who I am.

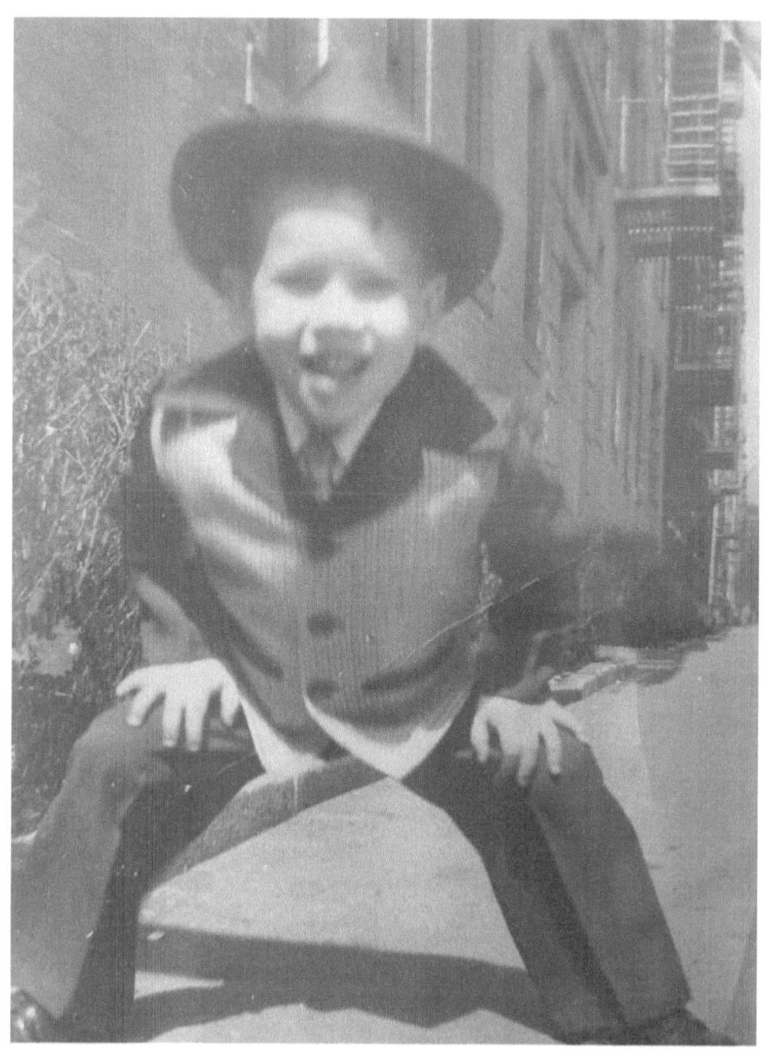

Ron Lemco in New York in the 1950s

CHAPTER 1

BRONX NEW YORK 1957

Officer O'Rourke. Try to envision the perfect Irish cop walking his beat. He could twirl his baton in a helicopter motion, first to the right then to the left, his hat was slightly tilted to the right side of his head. He knew most of the kids in the neighborhood by their first name and was what the kids considered a cool cop. O'Rourke let the kids pitch pennies to the curb and sometimes umped their stickball games that they played in the street. I once saw him hold back traffic for an important play. He was an older copy, in his mid- fifty's, but without the doughnut belly. For his age, he was in remarkable shape, and he was our neighborhood cop.

The 4th of July was approaching, and we kids had fireworks. They were illegal in the city, but Officer O'Rourke left us alone as long as we didn't do it in front of him. I was nine years old and loved firecrackers, as most of the kids did. Blowing up cans or playing chicken, seeing who could hold the firecracker the longest before explosion, were the general activities. The best, though, was called Dog Poop.

Anyone who had a dog in the neighborhood walked their dog in the street and let the dog do its duty. This was long before the days of the poop and scoop laws, so the poop would just lay there for days until eventually the huge monstrous city street sweepers would come wailing down the road and get rid of them.

Or...there were kids with firecrackers. Eyeful and ready to blow these piles of shit into kingdom come, hitting cars, or buildings, or just anything unlucky enough to be passing by at the time. We, the children of the neighborhood, had saved a cherry bomb we believed was close to a quarter stick of dynamite and had not yet found that perfect brown pile that deserved this magnificent piece of explosive. We blew up every pile on our block, and still, none were worthy of this prize.

Luckily, there was Mr. Swartz and his two Great Danes, as big as horses. Mr. Swartz lived in a small apartment with these two giant dogs, and we knew it was close to the time for Mr. Swartz to take his dogs for a walk. Patience is a virtue, and it paid off; this shit was worth it. We followed in anticipation. Sure enough, the first dog let go, and it was beautiful! I swear it had to have been a 2-pound drop. Not just that, but a work of art as well! The pile of Great Dane shit had the perfect design and looked exactly like a Dairy Queen ice cream type swirl with the twist and all at the end. It was perfect for the cherry bomb.

Now I am nine years old and maybe not the brightest kid in the neighborhood, and what was about to happen, I swear it wasn't planned. We had added two extra fuses to the cherry bomb, as we needed ample time to escape; we lit the fuse and ran. Then from around the corner comes Officer O'Rourke, just minding his own business. He sees a bunch of kids running, no doubt up to mischief, so he steps up his pace to see what we are up to. The cherry bomb explodes. I remember a piece of shit hanging from O'Rourke's lip.

His left side was consumed in dog shit, and it was hanging from his hat. Now, remember, I was nine years old, and this was the funniest thing I had ever seen.

As I said, I was not the brightest kid, and as I lay on the sidewalk, side-splitting from laughter, I see O'Rourke, who does not get the joke. Seeing him coming straight at me snapped me back to reality, but I knew he was old, and I could outrun him. As I began to run away, I looked back, and the old cop was running after me! That old man could run. I was no longer laughing, and I stepped up my pace. I looked back again, and he was still gaining on me. Now I was scared. I didn't know eyes could go that red. I gave it all I had, but it was not enough, as I felt a hand grab my hair and pull back with such unbelievable force that my feet flew out in front of me.

O'Rourke picked me up and sat down on a stoop and then put me across his lap and laid into my ass with his nightstick. I remember Mr. Swartz walking by with his dogs, and I yelled out, "Help me, Mr. Swartz!" He looked at O'Rourke, and his shit-covered uniform and said, "Hit him again." I took the beating like a man, but by the time O'Rourke was through with me, I, too, was covered with dog shit. I never knew if Officer O'Rourke ever forgave me.

One thing about growing up in the Bronx compared to kids who grow up in the country is that their imaginations very, a country kid seems to be supplied things to do, they differ from the city boy who pushes his imagination to the limit overcoming hot concrete and wall to wall buildings.

We had a clubhouse that we had built in an old sewer system. The system was still used for runoff in case of heavy rains. It was dark down there except for holes in the sewer caps; rats loved it down there.

The trouble with the rats they would eat our candles along with the fact city kids have no use for rats. My grandfather used to tell us that if rat comes out of the toilet, just scream, and they would run away. It was true the rats made the way from sewer pipes all the way up to people's toilet. Rats got into our food, always leaving a trail of droppings. Bottom line, we had no love for rats.

Now combine these facts with sadistic 10-year-old kid and the fact we had a few fishnets mix that with imagination, and we would capture the rats. We then would douse the rats with gas and bet which one would run the furthest before dying after we lit them.

Some made to a hole and escaped death somehow.

Now this whole story and its details were all needed in order for what is about to happen to fall in place.

AB was a close friend of mine; we all called him AB, which is short for Abraham. AB and I could not find our friends, and we thought they might be down in the clubhouse. AB said he had some matches, so off we went to the club.

A short background on AB who loved when we went down into the sewer for him to run ahead and hide behind a beam of something and jump out with a big BOO, which gave us a small scare the first10 times he did that, but it just made us laugh when he kept doing it for almost 2 years. But that was AB, and we just let him keep doing it.

So, AB and I climb down in the sewer, and what does he do but run ahead to hide. "AB, you asshole, you are not going to scare me, and besides, you have the matches!" I yell as he goes dashing off. I put my hand against the wall going slow, knowing AB is going to try and scare me. The only light are the beams coming from the sewer cap holes. And a beam hits what looks like a pair of eyes about 5 ft. in the air.

They do not look like human eyes, and I am a little scared when I yell out.

"AB, I see you, come on out," he does not answer I stretch my head looking at the eyes, which is starting to freak me out; I see a little red in them.

"AB, really, you're not scaring me. Come on out, I see you." I thought I heard a grunt, and then it seemed like a light beam followed what jumped down from a beam. It was the most ungodly rat I ever seen. I thought it weighs 100 pounds. Right away, my head started to think what this thing was that just thumped on the ground in front of me.

Like I say I am not the brightest kid on the block, but my imagination works just fine. I figure this is the Avenger Rat come for pay-back for the rats that we set on fire. I feel the rat already ate AB and is coming after me for dessert.

I flash back to what my grandfather had said," if you see a rat just scream." Well, I was in the Bronx they could have heard my scream in Yonkers. I found out right there that my grandfather lied to me. The rat had a slither walk was coming towards me looking at me with red eyes. I ran like a thief.

I made to the latter looking back to see if rat had followed me, but I didn't see it. I climbed out and went looking for the gang, I found them at Sarge's pizzeria.

"A hundred pound rat just ate AB, I mean it is a huge rat just ate AB," At first the guys just looked at me and laughed but when they saw tears in my eyes they did believe something happened to AB. They left to go check it out but not before one of the guys grabbed a chain and another a stick ball bat, they must have heard the scare in my voice to triggered fear in these guys.

We made to the sewer and we all went down in the tunnel. One of the guys had matches as he cautiously made his way forward with the rest of us behind him.

Now remember AB has been trying to scare us for years but to no avail. How AB got up on a beam I didn't know, but when he jumped down with a screaming Boo, well do you know that saying "shit your pants" A person can do that, I know I did.

The guys beat on AB for 5 minutes, but he never saw the Avenging rat, the guys never saw such a rat and to this day no one believes my rat story. I know what I saw.

CHAPTER 2

BI- POLAR

So, I go through mood swings. I have difficulties ranging way up and way, way down. My doctor tells me I am bi-polar. Well, this is how I analyzed it. I am human. Who doesn't go through mood swings or feel really good about their life and then go the other way? Doesn't circumstance decide mood?

I am going through my journal from 1973 to 1975 and I see how back then, before being bi-polar was a regular medical term, I sure had mood swings. My poems were simple, and they spoke of my feelings for the day that I wrote them. I read them now and I get bored with my so-called poetry. Here is a sample.

August 11, 1975

"WHY?"

Why am I the way I am, why do I do the things I do?

Does anyone really understand? Has anyone a clue?

Why do I have to explain my life or the way I chose to live?

I don't feel I am bad, rather than take, I choose to give.

People don't always know that you're real, you feel

That you love.

You must prove yourself no matter what you're thinking of.

Why am I even writing? No one will know what I say.

I have learned to accept it, that life is just that way.

Why does it hurt to express the real inner me?

Well, here is your answer. How do you explain free?

When I first began my journals, I would write like they were letters to God. Life makes people play so many games. In order to survive, you sometimes lose track of who you are. When I wrote, I wanted to be real and express my true inner- feelings. You cannot lie to God, so when I wrote, it was my truth, no need for games.

January 21, 1975

"JUDGE ME NOW"

Oh Lord I say to you with all of my heart

You are patient from me you never did part

I have done wrong so many times before

You would forgive me, but then I did more

And now a new chance you give me with ease

Now it is my turn for you to be pleased

The rest was in my hands, you showed me the way

If I did wrong from there, I think I should pay

So please forgive me for all the wrong I have done

Judge me now for I have just begun.

I was going through some funny times during this period of my life. I was in love with my third wife Becky, but we fought like cats and dogs. Every other week, she would go back to her mother's home in Albany, Oregon while I stayed in Tacoma, Washington.

I was raising Shane, my son, who was 6 years old. His mother, my first wife, Rose had died of pneumonia 4 years earlier. The Rose story will come later in the book.

"LASTING VISION"

Oh, power of the mind where is the peace I will find?
I keep looking, but wherever I turn,
It seems I have a new lesson to learn.
What is next? Is it my reason?
Or is it to come into another season?
Oh wind, don't blow me away for I so like it here.
Or is staying what I really fear?

Life is a struggle. I remember something I wrote when I was in the 8th grade. "Poor little Ronny sitting on a fence trying to make a dollar out of 99 cents." Now, years later I find that some things never change.

Money is gone the rent is due
Shelves are empty so what is new
I have been on the bottom I have been to the top
I have been the "JELLO", I have been the rock
I have seen the rainbow, I have felt the light
The rewards were so close, but I didn't fight

Then I developed a new frame of mind when I found a career that I was going to love.

Oh, it is here, the search is no more
Happiness contentment and money galore
A future, a hope, and a new frame of mind
Was here all along but just too hard to find

When Becky left this time, it really was over, and I missed her right off.

Love we had, but understanding never started

It is really sad for there was a lot there

A love I have had has now departed

But for my love, I will always care

She may return. Besides love, I am her friend

The love I had is still there…. it could never end.

My new career is taking off. I am the best salesperson in the company. I have recognition and money is no longer a problem. I am UP!

Oh, to be able to say I went all the way

Without quitting the awards were about to pay

I have stuck this long now and I had the drive

I was starting to feel I was really alive

Work without resentment is a matter of pride

I knew what I was looking for and took the stride

And it's nice to know you are by far the best

You're such an individual so unlike the rest.

I had replaced Becky with a slough of new women. It took away the craving for loving. I read back in my journals and saw the importance.

When you try to remember it is soon forgot

When you write it down you forget it not

To look back and know where you were last year

Gives you the feeling that for life you care

When you flash back to remember life's mistakes

You get answers now that are without the wait

The above is from the last page of my journal dated 2/17/75 to 3/23/76. Then I realized I had lost the journal I was writing in when I robbed the bank. This showed me what I had lost from April 1976 until the bank robbery on July 21, 1977. My brother, Larry, died of an overdose. I moved with my new company from Tacoma to Vancouver, Washington. I met and fell in love with Dee Dee Adler who was with me when we robbed the bank. (She insisted). I had lost all my feelings and emotions during that time. I am reminded what journaling means to me.

I do remember poker was my main source of income when I first moved to Vancouver. The upgrade to District Manager with my company was forgotten and I became lost in the land of the poker player. The lifestyle and money were more to my liking, they were also to become my downfall. Without my journal to remind me, all I had was my memory.

I knew I had to put aside money to take Shane on a promised trip to Disneyland and how much he was looking forward to going. I remember beating all takers in heads up poker. The bets range from $300 to $1000 per heads up match, winner takes all. I also remember thinking I was the fastest gun in the West. Then I ran into Don Bust, who had so much money and no fear. He busted me flat. I recall borrowing money from a loan shark to get back into poker and build my stash of money back up. I know when you need to win; luck has a way of going against you. When the loan shark gave me a gun and told me "get his money" and I also didn't have the money for Shane's trip to Disneyland, which was just days away, I decided to rob a bank.

"THE LAST"

Well the dream is over. It is clean out of sight.

Sobriety I gained and lost what was right.

I don't give a damn and I want to destroy.

My goal is to scam, but where is the joy?

Seems the world got cold and became mighty bad.

Seems I've lost my soul, now that's really sad.

So, what's it all about? All of the tripping before?
I wanted to scream due to not learning more.
I searched for what I thought I had found.
And as I looked around,
My face filled with sorrow as I headed out of town.

CHAPTER 3

EUGENE, OREGON

July 21, 1977

Dee Dee and I stopped in Eugene at a Denny's to grab a bite to eat. Our destination was Medford Oregon. We were going to rob a bank. There was no plan, nothing really thought out. I just knew I needed about $18,000 to pay back the loan shark, give Dee Dee $5,000, catch up on my rent, take Shane to Disneyland, and still leave me with $3,000 for a starting bankroll. Yeah, I did not want to get greedy.

I was wondering to myself what made me pick Medford, it sounded lucky. Medford, it had a good sound to it. Just go into the bank, flash my gun hidden in my belt, and hand the teller a note to give me $18,000. It didn't sound complicated.

We ordered our lunch at Denny's, and from the window I saw a US Bank across the street. As I headed to the bathroom, I saw a pay phone and stopped to look at the phone book. I looked up US Bank and found the number for the bank right across the street. I called the number and when someone answered, I said "I was in last week talking to the bank manager but forgot his name."

A pleasant voice asked, "Was it William Wolfe?"

"Yes, that's it," I said back.

"Would you like to talk to him?" the voice continued.

"No that's all right. I will come in and see him."

I went to the white pages and looked up a William Wolfe. There in black and white was his home number and address.

I called the number and a woman answered so I asked, "Is Mr. Wolfe in?"

She said, "No he is at the bank."

"Oh sorry, I will call him there." I responded back. And I hung up. I went to the bathroom and returned to the table just as our food was being served. I gave Dee Dee a kiss and told her "I got a plan".

It was as if I knew it would be our last day together. We got a room not far from the bank. I decided to live it up and get a nice room with a jacuzzi. We made love and then took a jacuzzi. The day was still young, but I decided to wait until the next day to use the plan. We drove to the coast. It was a beautiful day as we walked along the beach. The day was ending.

"SILENCE IS GOLDEN"

The sand slowly disappears, as four feet sink out of sight while pushing sand to the side.

Hands together with heart, head against shoulder.

Looking at the sun starting to smolder like a wax-less candle.

The endless look of silver with a golden beam.

The ocean and sun together as one, Except for them.

The beach is theirs and Gods.

Eyes meet. Their rhythm together, speaking in silence.

The power of the universe, the strength of time.

Speaking not in voices, just look for it comes.

It is the language of the heart.

Bodies meet to full-fill the craving of touch.

Ah, the heart skips a beat.

The feeling over coming with harmony.

The combination of two becoming one.

The magnitude of giving far surpassing the wanting of taking.

The swarming of vibrations. Stirring the blending togetherness.

*She looks at him in oneness and says "I've got sand
in my ass."*

Dee Dee is a beautiful girl, street wise for all of her 19 years. We kept running in to each other by chance talking a little each time, the third encounter I asked her out and we stayed together, from that day until the robbery. She was like a love I had never known. She asked nothing of me, and we just clicked. When I told her, I was off to rob a bank, she asked to come along. My biggest regret is that I let her. In her mind, I was some kind of gangster and she just believed in me.

"UNITY"

I remember this world when I was alone.

Feeling the loneliness, like having no home.

For home is where the heart is and my heart had no meaning.

*Existence was just another day while loneliness was
screaming.*

Come Love, Come Heart, Unite.

Then from a rainbow, love was sent. Feeling and knowing

This love was meant.

For love is a oneness, a blessed grace, power of the universe

The sender Fate.

Knowledge of the heart, feelings of the soul,

These blissful feelings let me know

We are love making our hearts recite.

Visions see what the future brings

Togetherness and wedding rings.

For love has brought us home never needing again to roam.

Love Came, Heart Came, United.

Once two, now one, lost pain forgetting sorrows,

Love Came, Heart Came, United.

I fell in love many times in my life, and I felt as I wrote. I ask myself have I really ever lived as I felt. Was I just a romantic that took the moment in time to make it all so glorious? No, it was real at the time that I felt it. I lived everyday as colorful as I could perceive in my mind. Am I phony? Not in my mind. Did I hurt people along the way because of the way I was? I am sure I did, but without intent.

"ACCOUNTS RECEIVABLE"

Borrowing from the bank of life we have all made the loan

It comes when we need it, giving is the only payback known

Some continue to borrow, making loans interest due

Payment just never forgets, every day comes a clue

The conscience receives bill, there are no bankrupts in giving

Leaving it all to your will and how you choose your living

This Lad borrowed to full extent kept putting payment off till tomorrow

Giving felt cheated of the rent thus, tipping the scales to sorrow.

What comes around goes around the bank of life keeps the books

For what I owe I now pay. Why Not? It is my debt.

CHAPTER 4

"THE ROBBERY"

Dee Dee and I drive by the address I found in the white pages for Mr. William Wolfe. There is one car in the driveway. We then drive three blocks to a Safeway store and park the car.

"Lady" I say to Dee Dee as I look right into her beautiful brown eyes. "You really don't need to do this, I am in this mess not you, and I can pull this off by myself."

She reaches out and puts her hand to my face, moves her lips to mine and after a long deep kiss, she says. "Let's do this thing. We have a Jacuzzi waiting for us".

"Are you sure babe? This is kind of crazy. I've got to do this, you don't", I replied back not knowing for sure if I would do this on my own... in fact, I was not too sure I wanted to, not that I was scared; I just knew how stupid it was... maybe I was scared.

"If you are doing it then so am I," Dee Dee whispers back.

I take a deep breath, reach behind the seat, and pull out a sack. I had my gun and the one the loan shark had given me. I handed a .22 pistol to Dee Dee then I place a .38 into my belt. I never told her that the guns were not loaded, that I didn't want to hurt anyone.

We walk the three blocks back to the home. We walk up to the door. It is very warm summer day, and the door is open with the screen door unlocked. The screen makes a little squeak as I slowly open it. A tiny little dog comes running at us with a high-pitched annoying bark. A lady comes around the corner and I grab her and put the gun to her head. I admired this woman right off as I told her to make her dog quit barking and she said, "Get them, Sic 'em!"

"Hey Lady, this is a gun at your head" I snapped back.

"What is this about, what do you want?" she talks which stops the dog from barking.

"Your husband's bank is going to get robbed," I declared as I started tying her hands behind her back.

"So, you're going to kidnap me?" she asked to the realization of what was happening.

"Something like that," I came back with as I led her back to the bedroom and saw a phone I was hoping would be there. "Now, Mrs. Wolfe I have no plans to hurt you, I will be calling your husband in a minute and I will let you talk to him. You just tell him what is happening, and I am sure it will all work out fine."

Dee Dee interrupted me showing me a jewelry box and said, "Look at all this shit, looks like the bank business is good".

"We are robbing a bank not people, put it back Baby" I replied, and Dee Dee did as she was told.

I picked up the phone and dialed the number to the bank. "US Bank, how may I help you?" asked the voice that answered. "Mr. Wolfe please" I asked, and the voice replied, "Please hold."

"This is William Wolfe. How can I help you?"

"Mr. Wolfe, be real calm. I have your wife as a hostage and will let you talk to her in a minute."

"What? Huh? Who is this?" he questioned back in a way that was anything but calm.

"Mr. Wolfe this is not a joke. Here… say hello to your wife and for her safety, calm down" I said in the firmest voice I could muster up. I then handed the phone to his wife.

I heard his voice say "Marjorie" and for the first time I knew what her name was.

"Hello Bill" Marjorie spoke into the phone. Mr. Wolfe knew something was wrong, Marjorie never called him Bill, but he knew her voice.

"You ok Marge?"

"Yes, I am fine. There are people here with guns Bill." was all Marjorie got out when I grabbed the phone back from her.

"Mr. Wolfe, do you understand this is no joke?"

"Don't you hurt her?" he said back in a demanding voice. "That isn't in the plans if you do as you are told, Mr. Wolfe."

"What is it you want?" he asked humbly as I started to convey the plan I was hoping would work, counting on human nature.

"Mr. Wolfe, I want eighteen thousand dollars in small bills no bigger than a twenty. I want you to bring it to your home and when you get there, you are to walk in and put your hands against the wall. You need to do this with in twenty-five minutes. Did you get all that Mr. Wolfe?"

"Yes, I will do that, but don't you hurt my wife!" he said.

"You or your wife will not be hurt, but Mr. Wolfe, I am desperate, and I feel for such a small amount of money you will not take the chance of any harm coming to either of you. Now, I am starting the clock Mr. Wolfe… you have twenty- five minutes." I hung up the phone.

I often wondered if I had not asked for all the money in twenties, would the plan have worked? Mr. Wolfe only had $12,000 in twenties at his branch and had to go to another branch he oversaw to get the other $6,000. That branch manager saw something was wrong and called the F.B.I. I was right about Mr. Wolfe not taking a chance for the little amount of money, and I was right about human nature. Mr. Wolfe could not help but act nervous. Which reinforced the other manager's instinct to make the call to the cops.

"RESCUE ME"

Wind of the night, through long day

And secrets you never tell

Come forth and say, you'll blow me away

From this piece of Hell

Remove the chain, of yesterday's strain

Pain I cannot ignore

Pain time inflicts, as bars restrict

Feelings I cannot restore

                                        What's Behind the Words?

A living tomb of endless doom
And me with no excuse
To gamble free on a spree my memories seduce
I played the game, no one to blame
For a crazy plight
But mighty wind, once my friend
Rescue me white night.

CHAPTER 5

"THE CAPTURE"

Mr. Wolfe came in the door and did as he was told and put his hands against the wall. He did not look at us. Lying beside him is a bank sack with $18,000 in twenty-dollar bills. I kept my gun pointed at him as Dee Dee tied his hands behind his back.

I asked him "Did you bring the police with you, Mr. Wolfe?" It was a stupid question, as if he would admit he did if he had. He replied, "No. Where is my wife?"

"She is fine; I will take you to her." I said as I lead him back to the bedroom and saw the relief in his eyes as Mrs. Wolfe smiled at him.

"Mr. and Mrs. Wolfe, I am sorry I had to do this and for any hardship I brought to you. It is nothing personal. May I have the keys to your car please?"

"In my right front pocket" Mr. Wolfe replies.

I reached into his pocket and said, "I will be taking your car." "No problem, take It." he spoke humbly.

Dee Dee and I left the house carrying the sack of money Mr. Wolfe gave us and got into Mr. Wolfe's station wagon.

"Look at this Ronny!" Dee Dee said in excitement as she opened the bag and flashed the cash in my face. "We did it! We did it!" she was acting like a little girl that just won a contest.

"Not over just yet, but yeah, that cash sure looks good" I snapped back to hold down Dee Dee's excitement as we pulled down the street. The feeling of accomplishment lasted only until I pulled to the end of the street. There, backing into a driveway, was an easy to tell un-marked police car with two men in it.

"Oh, shit Lady, that's the Man" I said between grinding teeth and then pushed the gas pedal to the floor.

I realized I was in a station wagon and no way could I outrun a police car, but I had to try something. I was doing about 50 miles an hour and looked to see the police car not far behind. There was a stop sign up ahead and a big truck coming fast down the main road I needed to cross. I hit the gas knowing there was no way to make it if the truck did not see me coming and apply his brakes.

It was like you see in the movies. The truck driver did see me coming fast, and he did apply his brakes and was skidding as I passed by within inches of being hit. The police car skidded to stop just inches from hitting the truck. They lost sight of us. We drove over a small hill then immediately turned left into an apartment complex. We jumped out of the car with the sack of cash just in time to see the cop car going by at a massive speed.

I looked up to the sky and said with the release of my breath "We lost them." Our car is right across the street.

Dee Dee is making her way to jump a fence. "No, let's get to the car while we can."

We headed across the street as three cop cars with their lights flashing came to a skid. The cops were out of their cars in seconds, and I heard the sound of shotguns pumping a shell into the chamber. I looked and saw barrows that looked the size of a baseball pointed right at me.

A voice commanded, "Do not move! Put your hands in the air!"

"Let's shoot it out." Dee Dee said, and God believe me she was serious.

What a woman! More balls than any man I ever knew, including myself. I froze like a punk as I remembered I never told Dee Dee that the guns were not loaded. I sure didn't want to hurt anyone.

"It's over Babe. Put your hands up." As always, she did as she was told. Thank God, because if she had made one move towards her purse to get the gun, they would have killed us right then.

In less than a minute we're put face down onto the ground, handcuffed and then placed into the back seats of separate vehicles.

We were being driven to jail when I heard a voice come across the radio. "Mr. and Mrs. Wolfe's children are missing. See what suspects know." I knew nothing about any children. The last thing in the world I would do is hurt a child. The cop in the front seat turns to me and said, "What do you know about Mr. and Mrs. Wolfe's children?"

My whole world had just crumbled. I am handcuffed in the back seat of a police car. I am going to prison for a long, long time. I did not know what I was thinking, but the words just came out. "What time is it?"

The statement brought the cop to life. "What are you saying Punk, you got their children? Are you an idiot? Right now, you're in trouble for a robbery, but if you mess with children, you are in some big trouble Buddy. I mean the death penalty. What do you know about those children?"

I come back like I am Tony Montana in Scarface. "I told that bank president not to bring the cops in, well now it is too late. Well maybe not… there is still time to save the children."

The cop car pulls into the Federal Building as I finished my gangster role play statement. The cop opened up the back door and showed me no mercy as he pulled tightly on my handcuffs and almost lifted me out of the car. He put his face right into mine and with his bad breath, he said "I will rip your face off punk, tell me where those kids are!"

The other cop pulls him off me and they hustle me into the building. I looked behind to see them leading Dee Dee between two cops. A third cop is holding the bag of money.

I am led into a small room and put into a chair. Two cops work on me. One grabs my hair as he screams into my ear, "Where are those kids? I will kill you with my bare hands if you don't start talking right now."

I always wanted to be an actor and here I was up for an Academy Award. I came back with a look in my eyes that I tried to transpose as some kind of evil. "Now if you kill me, that won't get the children back, will it?"

The cops looked at each other as one of them made a motion to walk out of the room, but not before he gave my hair a powerful pull. I watched as they made their way to what I figured was the commanding officer and told him the situation. After a minute, the big shot cop made his way to me in the room. He showed some moxey.

"Not a good day for you, huh Ron" he said in a mellow yet sincere voice. I am Detective McCloud."

"Well, it didn't take long to find out who I am, huh?" was what I found myself saying.

"Like I said, I am a detective," McCloud said with a snicker. His name made me think of the TV cop show with Dennis Weaver called McCloud.

"Want a cigarette?" he offered as I was thinking of good cop, bad cop. He, no doubt, was the good cop.

"Yeah, I really would" I said and without hesitation he took one from his pocket put it in my mouth and lit it.

"Tell me about the kids, Ron!" He looked me right in the eyes as I drew back a strong puff of my smoke. To that point I was not sure what I was doing about the kids myself. I just thought it as an ace in the hole. I also was wondering about the kids.

"They are safe for right now," I responded as I blew out my smoke.

"Safe, what do you mean by that, are the kids in danger, Ron? What is it you want?"

It was time to play my ace. "Ok, you see my lady out there handcuffed, she is just a young kid that I led astray. She doesn't deserve what I brought down on her."

"Alright, what about her?" McCloud was quick to respond as I went on.

"And you see that sack of money on the table!" I was saying as McCloud took the cigarette from my mouth, flicked the ashes on the floor and put it back in my mouth and said, "Go on."

As though it was a script, I came out with my demands.

"Ok, you give my lady that sack of money and let her go, you tell her to call me once she feels safe and that no one is following her. When I hear from her then I will take you to the kids." I finished with a quick look at McCloud right into his eyes.

He looked back with an intense stare. And I'll be damned if he didn't come right back saying "Give me a minute" and he left the room. He talked to the two bad guy cops a minute then went to the phone and made a call. As I saw it, he was going to call some bigwig F.B.I. person in Washington D.C. to tell them the situation and was going to be told to do as I asked, putting the kids as a first priority. The girl and the money were no problem. She would be easily found later.

Right about then a cop on another phone yelled out "The Wolfe children just came home safe; they were at a movie! That punk never had the Kids."

McCloud looked at me not in disgust but more like admiration and just said, "Good try Kid, I felt you were full of shit and when we found the guns you had were unloaded, well it never seemed you were out to hurt anyone."

As crazy as it was, and knowing I was in a world of trouble, McCloud made me feel good that he could see I was just stupid and mixed with circumstance. That was where I was right now and where I felt I was going to be for a long time.

CHAPTER 6

June 11, 2018

It is actually over ten years since I began writing this book "What's Behind the Words." It is like I have voice inside me telling me that I have a story to tell and who may listen really doesn't matter to me. I know going in that I am an unknown writer and that the book is never going to be a blockbuster. Maybe my grandkids will get a kick out of reading my life story and reading my so-called poems.

But half of writing is brought about by inspiration and with me this comes and goes. I have poker to play, Uber to drive and TV to watch and a hundred other reason's that inspiration disappears.

Life continues, my kids get older and now that I am almost 70 years old, I wonder if I will ever finish what I started. But sometimes inspiration comes out of nowhere. You don't look for it, but it kicks you into creativeness again, and you become inspired by someone else, you never think about this person until he died a few days ago.

Anthony Bourdain is the man that kicked me into the light again. After watching his documentary and remembering watching his show many times but never once realizing what an amazing man he was. He was world traveler, a chef, had a TV show (Parts Unknown), but most of all he was a Storyteller who expressed the purest inner being of a man, along with having a way with words that absorbed anyone listening. All great attributes that within my ego I feel I also have.

So, I begin writing again as I pulled out one of boxes filled with all my writings and poems and begin to hopefully not bore the reader in hopes you want to read the next page. That's if you can get by my grammar and spelling, thank God for spell check. Also thank you Anthony Bourdain for being a man's man.

FLASH BACK

August 1977

I'm in prison, they have given me a total of 65 years; 20 years for robbery, 20 years for kidnapping, 20 years for burglary, and 5 years for car theft. The parole board runs it all together into forty years, two 20-year sentences running consecutively. That means do the first 20-year sentence, then start all over with the second 20-years. I am 27 years old, so in my head I calculate I will be here until I am 67 years old.

"IF ONLY A DAY"

Once just a seed not knowing had a crave

Digging into the soil the only way it could behave

Far enough so the rain could find its way to penetrate

*With the strength of the sun and all the ingredients
to germinate*

The seed felt a change, a certain kind of power

Forgetting what it once was…. for now, it was a flower

Growing as tall and straight as nature had inbred

The pride to see it grow and fragrance spread

Upon the sands of days that ran so slow

Flowers why mourn for them or feel their woe

To follow its flowered destiny is without grace

A flower plucked and left to dry in a casket case…

I think of Dee Dee and how I messed up her life, she got 10 years for her part in my stupid escapade. That was part of my plea bargain, in pleading guilty, that Dee Dee would get a maximum of 10 years.

I feel Dee Dee deserves to be part of the book and I will let the letter she sent me on August 18,1977 give the reader an inside look of why she would follow me into the destructive course I took. It is a long letter, but the insight is needed along with the poem she wrote that ended her letter.

Hello my loving man,

I just received your letter dated the 16th; I am sorry you had to spend your birthday alone in this hell hole. Guess there will be many more lonely days to come.

Oh well they say good things don't last forever (ha ha) but bottom line I've accepted we messed up, so it is pay day.

For your sake Ron become nuttier than a fruitcake, it helps me over here with the women. This place cannot take away our laughs.

Ron. I always told you I wanted you to feel free and honest; I never told you I wanted to lock you in a cave. I was afraid you would have found it contradictory and not understand it. I am glad that you love me enough to understand. I do believe you love me Ron, it has to be love to reach inside me this far. I thought after the times in the past finding out how much love can hurt, so I do not think I fell in love with you blindly. I am sure I would have loved whether you loved me or not, but I would have kept up a wall to keep the distance. But you do love me and there are no mental or spiritual or distance or time or space that will kill the love I have for you. When fear creeps in I lash back and so far, I am winning the fear factor.

Ron, you have a very special beauty and meaning to me and I am happy when you say I inspire you. There is one part of our love hard to understand so I asked God for help but received no answers. I knew I would have to find the answers to what it was

I was looking for. If it was up to me, I would have kept my nose in the air and not given you the time of day. But God intervened as we kept running into each other in the weirdest places, so I took it as a sign from God and let us happen.

Now with us both locked up and you are searching for God, I am looking to get back to him we both have a common need. I believe there is a plan for us, and that God has been part of it. That there is just too much that happened to pass off on fate, that there is a definite purpose and plan for us and everything we are going through is all part of it.

Well, I will get this in the mail, keep your head up and stay sweet for me, keep searching for God.

Love you always, Dee Dee

Dee Dee's poem she wrote:

"Just us Three"

There are so many things I miss today
For your loving arms so far away
All the children for who I used to pay
The little apartment I used to stay
And my family I put to shame
Most of all I miss you my love
And all the things we have not done
Simple things that we could share
Like laying in bed without a care
All the things money can't buy
Our natural beauty even getting high
At the ocean watching the seagull fly
Or see the sunset and the watch it rise

Dee Dee had written me 100's of letters and today I opened the first box and there was her stack of letters to me. The one I just wrote was the first one I grabbed, and I think it was the perfect one. Like fate drove me to this letter, like we felt fate brought us together, or as we believed at the time that it was God's doing.

But here is the whole point of the chapter; time and change are the master of all things. I have no doubt that we loved each other but time brings change. Dee Dee found love with other women, no doubt my fault as I put her in that situation, I wrote my second novel called "Women of Circumstance" and it deals with the circumstance of 4 different women and why they ended up in prison, Dee Dee was part of every character.

Within a year I had married my 4th wife Jodee and moved on somehow rejecting the love I still felt for Dee Dee. As I write this today, even though it has been 40 years I realize that what Dee Dee and I had was very special and I still have a place in my heart for her.

I have tried to locate her many times, once when I received a big settlement and wanted to see if I could help her out financially, but I had no luck.

Jodee who I married in prison was a phase, yet during the time in prison I loved her. I thought to the utmost, but the old saying you don't know someone until you live with them, proved to be true. Or is that a cop-out to the fact I met Valarie. And now 37 years later I am still with Valarie and still in love. Was she the one they call perfect love, was it the five children we had together, was it the acceptance of each other's weaknesses, or the way we make each other laugh? I really don't know the answers other then we have always been best friends.

Bottom line I'm not sure what love is, I sure had my chances. Like Shane, my first son, the one Dee Dee ends her poem with how much I loved him, that fatherhood lasts forever, now he is 48 years old, and we don't get along, how does that kind of love die, or is it just on hold?

That same box I pulled out had four albums of photos covering my prison years and Shane growing up. How many times I cried myself to sleep thinking of him and the love I had for him, the sorrow I felt for him with his Mother dead and his Dad in prison.

How has the years made that all change? Does it just get lost or forgotten or is it you just move on with life taking everything as it comes, and that which is hurtful is rejected in defense of you surviving so you can be as happy as you want to be.

Well, I guess I will end this chapter and go pull out another box and let my mind take over the memories produced by that which is in front of me at the time.

CHAPTER 7

1995-1996

I am not sure if how I am going about writing this book is going to make sense. I already wrote 2000 words today which is twice as much as my goal of writing 1000 words day was, but it is like I am charged up and just want to go as long as my mind wants to keep going.

I went to my closet where I keep all my writings and reached and grabbed one of many journals, and I pulled out 1995 through 1996. Ok, so I believe that fate guides me, so with that as my excuse let me start my new chapter.

The book starts off with Valarie and myself opening up a new business in Buckley Washington called Consignment Center. With very little money to work with it would take a concept like Consignment Center for us to pull off a business. This is the concept: we sell other people's items they want to sell; we take their items on consignment and take a 25% of the selling price. We tried washers and dryers, furniture and many items that turned out to be more trouble along with running out of inside space it became more hassle than it was worth. But cars and trucks took off like a rocket and the selling price was much higher and our percentage of 25% of a $1000 to a $5000 per car gave us a bank roll within two months. We had to get an Auto Sales license which also gave me all I needed to go to the auto auction and buy cars wholesale. All of the sudden we owned a car lot. Having been in the sales end of selling cars and not to brag, but I was always the top salesman for the last ten years and well I had found my home.

My Dad has been in the hospital for twenty days now, he had an aneurysm. It has to be pure horror for him. He has lost use of his legs, they had to take out his colon, and he needs to have dialysis three times a week. He is 73 years old, and his loves are eating and playing poker. He now will not be able to do either.

He has been married to my mom for 49 years; they produced five children and had many grandchildren. With the pain he was in, and what he had to look forward to, the care that he would need, he chose the same as I would of.

Saul Lemco age 73 World War II Veteran, born July 16th, 1921 died today March 12th, 1995

My dad was a pretty simple man who met my mom in Australia during World War II in 1944. He was a great father who made all his kid's sports worthy by playing baseball, stickball and handball and ping pong. He also taught me how to play chess. He took care of his family and though we were never rich with money, we were never hungry or lacked new shoes, and we were rich in having great parents.

I need to write a special poem for the Old Man. The poem would have to bounce as he did through life. His days fighting in the ring, his one appearance at Madison Square Gardens, gave him a walk of his own. I spend many hours with Dad with him teaching me to box, which came in handy many times in the lifestyles I had chosen. For sure came in handy growing up in the Bronx and the time I served in prison. He had a good voice and could pop out a song anytime of the day. I sure miss my dad.

"HEY THERE BUDDY"

We can still hear you singing in your Frank Sinatra form.

We have you on tape with all your silly little songs.

I inherited from you the fact I like to sing

I play pretty good chess because you taught me some things.

And ping pong is my road game, you tossed me the ball.

It was you who instilled in me to get up when I fall.

What I learned most important was your spatiality

Everything in life comes in second right after your family.

And you might have tried to hide it, but you never could to me

My whole life whenever I saw a hero,

It was your face I would see.

**We always loved you Dad.*

There is one fact about life that is always 100% of happening that will be death.

It is funny that all the quotes my dad used over the years all the little idolisms he would tell me all my life; it was not until after his death that I remembered them. And that I use them and lived by many of them. Which I am sure inspired the following poem.

"SOME ADVISE"

Fly away, cry away, it is your choice which way want to go

Laugh and win or die in sin it is you who writes the show.

Flow & glow or strain in pain it is what you have within

Cash in the chips or lay in shit the winners take the bad with a grin

Coast downhill or crash and spill, it's you who takes the steps

See the good in the bad or go home sad, it's you who pays the debts.

So read between the lines or end up blind, fate is in what you make

Through the lessons of years and many tears

It is what you give not what you take.

March 27, 1995

We had a memorial service for dad today it was as nice as it could have been. We laid his ashes in the back yard under a head stone provided by the Veterans Administration that simply read: His name, date of birth and death, World War II

Vet, and a Star of David. All the family was there along with what friends my dad still had, and it finalized the end of a life. I looked around and saw 20 people that were there that never would have been if my dad had never existed. So just maybe it was the beginning of life.

My business is lacking because of the enemy in life, the thing I robbed a bank for, the thing that sent me to prison, the thing that cost me a couple of marriages, the thing that separated me from my son. Poker! God damn poker.

"BETTER DECIDE"

Seems the answer is easy you can almost reach out and touch

Those little answers yet they mean so very much

They provide solving problems with an idea to the head

By quitting the wasted hours to bring a brainstorm instead

But if it is so damn easy then come right out and say

The final solution and its map is right in your way

But you choose the game you're playing in your life of getting by

You could have had some answers but you never really tried.

I wonder what brought on that poem, it just blurted out, but I think it is about business and the fact you better come up with a game plan and applying yourself. It really narrows down to you ol' boy. If the Consignment Center fails, then you fail. It is about you being mature enough to get back to business. Have your plan, have your goal, now work it. Or is all this about why worry? Oh Ron. Get your head out of your ass.

CHAPTER 8

June 28, 2018

The last time I wrote was about how poker had messed me up so many times in my life, the reason it has been three weeks since I wrote is because I have been at the World Series of poker in Las Vegas all this time. And guess what?

I came home broke. I could spend my time telling you all the bad beats I had in three weeks. I could tell you I came in the money three times, coming in 11th out of 1260 players in the 1pm deep stack, a $250 buy in that ended up paying me $2700, and only ten players away from $40K, and the bad beat that took me out of the running, but I won't waste my time because the bottom line was that I lost. The other two tournaments that I got in the money came to another $2700. I had my old friend Seymore Flop back me for $5000 only to give him back nothing for my entries into the big events, bracelet events. They cost $1000 up to $1500 each to enter, never once getting close to the money.

I could tell you that the sickness was so bad that I borrowed $2500 from the Rio Casino who had given me a $5000 credit limit with them. How my daughter Destiny loaned me the money to pay the casino back. How I received a flash back to 1977 when I robbed a bank to pay back a loan shark, I owed money to.

But a sick mind thinks strange and the thought of last year at the World Series and coming in 36th out of 18,000 and winning $27,000 and winning a deep stack of $10,000, losing back half of my winnings before I came home but I did come home $16,000 up, well I thought I could do it again.

Not this year. But after forty-one years maybe I have matured as I have no plan to rob a bank.

Am I just a loser, am I a creature of habit? I must admit the three weeks there was like being in Disneyland for me. The twelve hours of peeking at my cards, the hopes of getting a good flop, the agonize zing re-appraisal of should I of played the hand I went out with differently.

I think I aged five years in the last three weeks for lack of sleep, the hours of sitting at the tables, the crap I ate, as well as the emotional ups and downs of gambling.

I thought of my baby girl Destiny who invited me to her 25th birthday party and when she found out I was in Vegas, she understood I wouldn't be there. It made me think of all my kids who had grown up with the fact that poker came in first place, over my kids and my wonderful wife, which they just accepted that was the way it was.

As I write this, I see what an idiot I am and have been and now in this state of mind of have given up poker again, that I will continue to work on this book. That I will go back and drive Uber again.

I have no money, but I am not behind on bills and the house payments are up to date. I get my $1200 social security and my wife has a good job; I will pay back Destiny the $2500 and I will just coast along as I always have done knowing everything will work out fine. And Seymour Flop and his

$5000 are gone and like he told me today. "We took a gamble and lost; we will get them next time" besides Seymour is a millionaire he won't miss the five thousand.

Writing has a way of taking away what is bothering me. It is like once it is written I can forget about it. Is that a cop out? I don't know but I feel like there is a load off my shoulders. I can accept that. Now I will do what I have to do to make up for my plight. Bottom line I loved the last three weeks, I think I am retarded.

Now I will just plug out a poem about what I just wrote. And maybe as the reader you can see what's behind the words means and understand what I am trying to transpose in the poem.

                                          What's Behind the Words?

"DEJA VU"

Oh these silly roads I always take ending up in the same place

I try to do each differently I even throw in some simple grace

*I go around the curves speeding but I feel like I am in
full control*

I think I have all the answers but in my heart I just don't know

And up ahead is a stop sign but I only yield to the right of way

*I may end up with a ticket but I chose my path, so I guess
I will pay*

*The road is close to ending and I will keep doing just
as I please*

*And my story will come to the end, kind of like
Thelma & Louise.*

Sometimes when I begin a poem, I have no clue where I am going with it, I have no ending and no vision really how it comes out. The poem above was written in less the 10 minutes and like most of my poems I am not sure how I like it, but like all my poems I never go back and re-edit them as I feel the time that I wrote was just how I was feeling, and there is an acceptance in being who I am.

Are you bored with this book yet? Does it make any sense? I wonder from a reader's point of view if anyone really cares how some other person feels. Sorry for the interruption, I ended 3 weeks ago with my journal from 1995-1996. So, I will start off where I left.

CHAPTER 9

July 29, 2019

Not true, it is over a year since I have written anything. The last time I took a break it took Anthony Bourdain's death to get the inspiration to write again.

Not sure what brought me back to the typewriter again, but here I am working on a never-ending book. How much I will write this time will depend on my attitude. Is it that I get bored with myself or do I just lose interest, ability, attitude?

Maybe there is something that takes over my desire to write. Right now, I am writing this for myself more than the reader and I look for reasoning and the understanding of just who the hell am I?

What have I done in the last year? Do I need to tell you that poker took up fifty percent of my time? I won $30,000 gambling in 2018, $29,000 in tournaments, $9230 playing in live games and losing $7810 playing stupid slot machines.

Anyone that plays slot machines has a slight touch of retardation, being a gambler, I know this. I wonder what the infatuation is with them dumb slots, knowing I am giving up my edge, knowing the casinos are built by slot players, but I keep playing them.

I am in the Diamond category with Caesar Casino's, about 10 different casinos which comp me free rooms, free food, and free show tickets. I love to flash my Diamond Card and move to the front of the line on shows and food lines. I enjoy being first on the list to play in the poker rooms. There are some benefits but if I took the $7800 it cost to get that status, I could have paid for more rooms then I used. But I am what I am, and I will continue to seek gratification from them stupid slots. And true I do hit some big pays which seems to make it worthwhile. It is like playing golf, I play funky all day but those one or two shots I make where I sink a 40-foot putt or hit a 5-iron from 150 yards out and get ten feet from the flag, that make it worthwhile to play. Does that make sense or am I just trying to justify my slot play? It is funny how I play games with myself.

Let's see besides poker, I have watched a bunch of news which I call the Trump show. There is a new story every day. I mean a pro writer could not come up with the stories that have come out every day for the last two and half years. I am not a Trump supporter; is about all I want to say to stay away from politics.

I don't sleep well and besides TV I have my phone and play a lot of Chess with other people and the same with "Words with Friends" which is how I finally fall asleep promptly around 5 am. But I don't come home from the Muckleshoot Casino until after midnight.

I played again at the 2019 World Series of Poker and stayed in Las Vegas over a month total. I had one good score in The Million Maker $1500 buy-in that had 8800 players and I came in 131st for a payout of $8900. I hit a few of small deep stack tournaments for another $5000, but bottom line I missed in many buy- ins, some $1500 a few $1000, many $500 and $600 buy ins, so the real bottom line after a month in Vegas I came home with $1000 less then I went there with. Of course, if I did not play slots, I would have come home a winner. Oh well, the sickness, but I got enough points to keep my Diamond status for 2020.

Two days ago, I came home from an 8-day vacation in Hawaii with the wife and all her siblings, had a blast, but now it is over.

Overall, it has been a good year even though I am behind $2900 in 2019 in my gambling so far. But mostly I am living the dream with Valarie my wife working for the airlines and getting free flights anytime I want to go somewhere. My free-wheeling lifestyle and to confess I am more content in my 70th year then I have been in my life. It doesn't get any better than being content.

And now back to the book I am supposed to be writing. I am not sure how to begin but wait that is enough to have a reason to write a poem.

What's behind the words started off with trying to get the reader to see or feel what the poem is trying to transpose, hence?

"WHAT'S BEHIND THE WORDS?"

There is a reason that feelings bring about attitude for a poet to be

Something that rips into the soul that somehow brings about reality.

I have overstated myself as a poet as I look for the next rhyme

I am sure I could do so much better; it is like I don't have the time.

What is it I try to prove? As I just find a way to fill in the blanks.

Am I blessed that words just pop in my head, to whom do I say thanks.

Or is it a curse that leads me down roads that have no real end.

Has my writing become my enemy, or is it a genuine friend.

This poem was not what I had in mind as I began to write tonight.

But the words are now written, whether it was wrong or right.

And I don't ask for forgiveness for things I cannot control

For the paths that I take are the places I come to know.

So I will end tonight's poem with hopes that there are some words of wit.

But for all I know from my past and all I done, that this is all a crack of shit.

So, there is another poem, and I can look for what to write next from my journals. But I need to research what to do next, but do I really need to? It is my book I can jump back and forth, go sideways or just whatever comes to mind. I just don't want to repeat myself. I will quit for tonight and go back and see what I have done to date along with editing. One thing I know for sure is editing is never over. My last two novel's required editing, editing, and when you were done editing, well then it was time to edit. And when the copy of the book comes out, people who read it will still wonder who the hell edited this thing. Oh well, I will do my best.

CHAPTER 10

July 31, 2019 1:35 A.M.

I just got home from the casino going out in 9th place, it paid seven spots, and so after six hours of play and the $120 it cost to enter, well I just lost the $120. I went out again when I could have kicked back and outlasted two players and would have won $200 for 7th place and up to $1600 for 1st place. But NO! I get A/K the most overrated hand in Texas Hold'em. Three players call $3000, and I am on the (dealer) button and I decide to try to steal the pot, so push in all of my $60,000 in chips I have. Except there were still the two players in the blind who have not acted on their hand. Well, the small blind snap-calls with his pair of Queens, and even though it is an even money draw, I lose when no ace or king comes. I am out.

So here I am on the computer after I find my journal dated 7/2/1979 until 1/29/1981. It is my prison journal two years after my sentence of 40 years. Two years I have survived and advanced in the understanding of life. But I am still in prison and still have much to learn.

Many people are infatuated with prison from books or movies they have seen, and I am here to tell you, or I guess my journal will be telling you, that prison really has nothing glorious about it.

I open my journal with; *I dedicate this book to my wife Jodee for she is doing this time with me.*

Hello, my name is Ronald (NMI) Lemco. I am 31 years old and 15 days; I like talking, singing, and sex, which I have done without now for over two years. I believe in live and let live, though' I don't always do as I believe. It is only about nine minutes before the lights go out, so let's get to the point of tonight's writings. There is so much left of life yet and prison is not your end but more of your birth to a whole life yet to come. (End of journal speaking)

I am in reality now looking at my writings and the feelings I was going through during the prison part of my life. I haven't really given prison much of a thought in the past thirty-five years as it seems like ten lifetimes ago. But now with my journal in front of me it comes back to life. I did good time, I used it wisely knowing I had no choice and acceptance to what had to be done, and I would just do. When I come to the poems I wrote, they seem to express something different.

"AND THE DAY BEGINS"

The day begins just minutes ago, what it will bring I wish to know

I am sure no surprises or even a special wish, just some words to remember this.

Darkened walls with lights atop, forty feet away freedom stops.

I cry somewhere from deep within, yet yesterday ended with a grin

It could have been worst you know it so, what if love was not part of this show

Then time would creep into these rancid days, you would have no time for praise.

I finished that poem before lights went out in less than nine minutes, so it shows I do not put much thought to my poems, they just slip out as fast as I think. It is like love in my life, very confusing by what I wrote, and I quote"

I wrote Dee Dee today still telling her how much I love her. Well, I didn't lie. I will always love her I also tell her in the future I see the two of us even though I am married to Jodee. I also write when it is love I am looking for it is Jodie's face I see.

Then I write Jodee and tell her of my love for her, but it is Dee Dee I masturbate to each night. Not every night as I use my third wife Becky and think of the antics, we did together in our short 3-year marriage. Yes, I still love Becky also.

Well, I told you I was confused.

I gamble every day in prison; we play for cigarettes. I play dominoes, pinochle, gin rummy or bet on the ping-pong game. I have become quite a good player in anything I play and have no problem supporting me and my celly Bobby with all of what we call Zoo Zoo's and Wham Whams, or in English, food, and smokes from the commissary. Not that you need much in prison, in actuality the food in prison is not that bad and is full of nutrition with balanced diets.

We have a clique in prison me Bobby, Billy, Pauly and Jesse and the most disgusting man you will ever meet, and we have named him Maggot. We watch each other's backs and as a rule we are left alone. We work out together in the weight pile and we are all in great shape. Bobby is exceptional and his strength is unbelievable. I found out once when he pissed me off and I punched him in the face. Bobby just shook his head grabbed me by the neck lifted me off the floor with my feet dangling and said, "Are you out of your fucking mind, I can snap you like a twig", and he put me down gagging.

He smiled and then said, "You got balls."

I snapped back "Fuck you, you're going to have snap my neck cause if you piss me off again, I will punch you again."

Bobby and I had a closeness that was unique after being in the same cell together for over a year. I took good care of his needs when it came to smokes or cupcakes and all such things as he had no outside family that would send money.

Oh, let me answer what is running through your head right now, No, we never had sex; we were just close, like brothers.

Bobby saved my ass a few times, one time when some convict who had lost more than he could pay to me in a gin rummy game. The convict out of some mind-set of survival thought I would come after him and that he needed to act first and was coming up behind me with a shank (a prison made knife) and was about to stick me when Bobby grabbed him a threw him off the second tier. The convict after getting out of the hospital from a broken shoulder stayed in PC (protected custody) the rest of his stay and there was no more trouble with him again.

Prison does have a way to bring you to reality, knowing that this was going to be your world that you are here for a while, now deal with it. The Novel I wrote called "Rest Stop" on Amazon came about because of the 40-year sentence I first received at my first sentencing. I had made a deal with the Prosecutor that he could do whatever he wanted to me, but Dee Dee was to not get more than ten years.

When it sunk in that I was going to be in prison for what seemed the rest of my life, well, I could not accept it and I thought about escaping. Bobby who was doing a life sentence for killing the man who he thought had raped his wife, only to find out his wife had lied, was with me on planning an escape.

No one had ever escaped from Oregon State Prison, so this was not going to be easy. Bobby and I would lie on our bunks and fantasize that if we did escape what would be the plan. For months we each threw out different ideas and then I came up with what I thought was the perfect plan.

"I got it Bobby," I blurted out when Bobby woke to the bell that goes off for breakfast. I had been up all-night thinking about the plan.

"What do you have Wizard?" That's what Bobby called me after all the things I had pulled off while behind bars.

"OK, I have driven to Las Vegas a few times and on Highway 15 there is the last rest stop before getting to Vegas. People stop there and pee and it is secluded. People have their pockets full of money they are taking to gamble with. So, we take over the rest stop, rob the people and save them all a trip to Vegas and get out of there with maybe forty grand in an hour's time."

"Yeah, sounds good, best of ideas yet anyway, let's go eat breakfast," was Bobby's response.

Well, the escape never happened but the idea stuck with me and twenty years later I would write my novel on the premise that if we had escaped what would have happened.

I remember the first poem I wrote in prison:

"HELL"

Laying here I look around, I will tell you what I see

It is a sliding door and sixteen bars stopping me from free.

*It is a six by seven foot room with a sink and a toilet on
the floor.*

I have already read forty times all the writings on the wall.

Looking around this rancid place I realize I am in jail

They described it in the bible but instead they called it Hell

Fed through the bars food not fit for a pig,

Oh, I wish I had a shovel for a tunnel I would dig

A bull walks up and down the hall asking "How do you do?"

When deep inside his ugly heart he doesn't care about you.

Ten minutes a day you get to walk the corridor

You better save your problems; the bulls have heard them all

The real joy every second day because of the rule

They let you take a shower, but don't forget to say thank you.

Down the hall is the hole they use it as a threat

Just to show you there is a worst Hell yet

Laying here I look around, I will tell you what I see

A place I can't adjust to a place not for me.

Yeah, the first twenty days at O.S.P. (Oregon State Prison) is spent in orientation and the poem describes what your day is like. I guess research needs to be done in those twenty days to see if someone in the prison will try to kill you or visa-versa. If you are a rapist or a child molester, they need to know if you can be put in with the population or need to do your time in protective custody.

I had just come from Lane County Jail where I did my crime. Court was held there and until I was sentenced that was where I would be. Boy, once I was released into population and given my own cell, I hadn't realized how bad county jails are, I would rather do a year in the joint then a month in county.

When I first realized that if I think about time, time will be the one in control, I had to find some kind escape from reality as I looked at a forty-foot-high wall. I mean I robbed a bank and got caught so I deserved to be where I was at but now, I had to deal with it in a way I could handle my situation, and this is what I chose.

On the other side of the wall were monsters, dinosaurs, things that would do me harm. On this side of the wall, I was safe the wall protected me. Sound pretty simple, well it worked for me.

"THEIR BODY, MY MIND"

Crazy man crazy, it's all insane. Crazy is part of this domain.

I make visions that can't be true appear; amusing me is my new career.

The slightest thought can be a clue; with my mind I can see any view

Women of beauty, so debonair, for my lustful thoughts they prepare

The brain is strong and easy to persuade my mind to be carried from this stockade

I move to an island in another hemisphere, to reality I am a mutineer

My body is theirs to captivate, but my mind they will never penetrate

And that is what you do if you want to survive prison life. You must forget what you always took for granted, FREEDOM. What a powerful word that is and the old saying," You don't know what you have till it is gone." It is so very true. To open up a fridge door, turn the TV to what you want to watch, even turn your own lights off and on at your will. And the big one sex, oh God, do I miss sex.

Point is you can't think about it or it will kick your ass, so I don't, and I survive. I think out of the 2500 inmates that are at O.S.P. I think I have got it the best; I am activities director, and my only job is to clean a closet. I announce all the shows, I have access to phones, and I sleep every day until noon. I manage my own softball team, I call the Mean Machine, after the Burt Reynolds movie The Longest Yard.

I bring stars into the prison when I get Barbara Mandrel and Country Joe and the Fish who are booked at the Salem State Fair to come to the Prison, and they do a charity show. It makes me a hero with many of the boys. I get to play pool or ping pong up in activities all day long if I want. I work out in the weight pile with boys every day and I am in the best shape of my life.

I get along with all the different cliques. The Aryan Brotherhood, Uhuru a Black Group, the Mexicans; they all accept me as just a cool guy. I have some of each on my softball team mostly lifers, I don't care who you are, if your good you get on my team. Lifers have plenty of time to practice. I prove it by us winning most of our games. For a prisoner I am living the dream. I am quoted as saying. "If there would have been women in prison I would still be there."

Warden Cupp once called me to his office and asked me to help out on a dispute going on between the Whites and the Blacks since I had each leader on my soft ball team. I talked to them, and shit was going to come down over a carton of smokes over a basketball bet, how stupid I thought. I wanted to please the Warden and maybe have a favor owed to me and for the small price of two cartons of smokes I ended the dispute by giving each side a carton.

I think I was paid back by the Warden a few months later when I had to go to their Kangaroo court over a write-up I received. No one is found not guilty when it came to a convict's word against a prison guard's word in this court system they have inside the walls. Well, I was to become the exception. But I must admit, I think I earned it.

I was playing dominoes with one of the boys when the bell lunch rang. Inmates have 5 minutes to get across the control room floor and into the lunchroom. Well, my buddy and I finish the hand of dominoes and I have to take the dominoes back to my cell. I guess I was one or two minutes late walking across the control room floor, when a prison guard stops me and asks why I am late. Oh man, I don't need this shit; I just came out with what popped in my head. "I was passing out towels!" was what I replied, knowing that orderlies pass out new towels during the lunch period. I was thinking the guard would know the procedures and the conversation would be over.

I thought it worked when the guard, came back saying. "OK, get to lunch."

Only the guard was not as stupid as I thought he was. I guess he knew who I was and called my cell block and found I was not an orderly. When I came back from lunch there was a write-up waiting for me on my bed. Shit, I thought as I opened up the write-up and I was charged with two infractions, Disobedience of an order, and Lying to staff.

You got to be kidding me, they got murderers and rapist along with 2000 other scum bags, and I get a write up for lying to staff.

Now it becomes a hassle because I am in the honor block and if you get a write-up and are found guilty, you must move out of the block. There is a six month wait before you can apply to go back to A-block (honor block). It is nicest place in the joint to be, we have play tables, open showers any time of the day, a TV with our own remote control, cells that remain open, and you are able to come and go as you please. And the fact that Bobby and I would be separated and just moving all your stuff to go to a block that just comes with a cell. Yep, bummer, but it is what it is.

It works out funny as my court date is the same day that I am going to marry Jodee. My wedding is at 11 am and court is at 1 pm. The wedding goes nice and is over fifteen minutes before my court appearance.

Booby had been working on getting some killer weed called Maui Wowi and it had been a couple of weeks since I had been high. Bobby has a joint rolled when I show up at the cell. "Cool"

I reply. I am going to need that after court I say as Bobby offers it to me to smoke before going to court. "I can't go to court high."

"Sure, you can." Bobby says. "You're going to plead guilty, right, how hard can that be? You can plead guilty high."

I think about it for about two seconds and say, "Sure why not." Wow, it took no time for the weed to kick in, I didn't care what the name of the weed was, it took hold, and I was buzzed instantly. I almost got lost trying to find my way to the court room.

I showed up and was about to sit on the bench with other inmates who have their hearings, when the door opens, and my name is called. I walk into the court room and who do I see but Warden Cupp who is one of the four Judges. Oh man, no shit, this is not my day.

"Mr. Lemco you are here today for two violations; Disobedience of an order and Lying to staff, how do you plead?" Captain Numura asks, one of the four also on judge panel. I always got along with him. It was right then that idea came into my head. I am thinking a misunderstanding; yeah, that is how I will play this. My mind is racing what rhymes with towels, how's no, cows no, oh I got it, yes, yes perfect.

Just then my thoughts were interrupted by the Captain. "Mr. Lemco we are waiting for your plea!"

I started talking right off the top of my head hoping that the weed high hadn't disillusioned me. "Well, I assure you this whole thing is just a misunderstanding, you see I was... "

Just then I was cut short by the Captain again. "Mr. Lemco, how do you plead?"

"I guess not guilty!" I reply. "Ok, tell us your version."

"I was trying before you interrupted me." Oh, geez why did I say that, looking at the four faces in front of me who were wondering the same thing.

"Just tell us your story; I can't wait to hear it," the Captain snapped back.

As I looked at Warden Cupps face he had an amused look on it. "Ok, I am sitting on the pot when the lunch bell rang, sometimes you can't rush, Mother Nature, and I was a few minutes late going across the control room floor. The officer stops me and asks why I am late for lunch. Well, I tried to be as eloquent as possible, I didn't want to say I was taking a shit, so I said I was passing my bowels. I didn't say I was passing out towels, I'm not even an orderly, I don't pass out towels."

I am looking at the panel and all of them; I mean all of them could not hold it after one of them began to laugh. The looks I got were almost like admiration, like I just made their day. They pull themselves together and one of them said go into that room please Mr. Lemco. There is a small room they send the convicts to wait while they all discuss their opinions and come up with a verdict.

I have my ear against the door, and I hear a mumble, "Like the little son-of-a-bitch is lying through his teeth, but I love the story," they are still snickering.

After a minute or two they call me back into the room. "Mr. Lemco this is your lucky day as we heard you got married this morning. In fact, if your story is true, you would have been lying and you would have been excused under the conditions of why you disobeyed an order. Not that one of us believes your story, but under all the conditions and the fact that there is no way to prove your story is false, we find you not guilty.

"Thank you," I replied as I looked at the Warden who had a look like, we are even for the favor you did for me. I was ok with that.

Time if you let it can creep by, I am in my cell thinking of poem I can dedicate to time. That time is really the master of all things and outlives everything.

"OLD MAN TIME"

*You do exist, well then, I ask you this, are you a
friend of mine?*

Do you control all, journey for evermore; is the wind your wife?

Well tell me this, or did you miss, in your last blink

How you rule all, cities fall, fossils and mountains sink.

*You make babies grow; you melt the snow and make
wrinkles show*

It is August in a prison surrounded by concrete. The temperature is close to 100 degrees; combine that with concrete and you are sweating all day long. They have air conditioning, but it doesn't kick in until 80 degrees. If you go out to the yard there is no shade, for shade would mean some kind of concealment and the gun towers need a view of every inch of the prison.

Temper's flair up and at the drop of a hat and there is trouble. There have been two stabbings this week alone. I have seen three fights in the yard this week and two fights in the chow hall. It is not only the convicts that have grown tempers so have the prison guards. An inmate is having a conversation with a guard, not sure what happened but the guard hits the inmate with his club. The inmate defends himself and hits the guard in the face. Within ten seconds, five guards join in with their clubs wheeling on the inmate.

This is happening in front of 300 inmates. The riot begins.

"HOT SUMMER DAY"

All builds up with times corrosion
Until finally that hate brings about explosion
Looking at changes that will unlock the gate
Striking out at whatever for the inner hate
Most follow a leader or two
Each watching what the other will do
Yelling demands that are out of line
Breaking the monotony of unchangeable time
Ripping apart the badge without a face
Only to have another take his place
The hate between the Races time has come
It was destined to happen but it has just begun
White on black until red is shown
Beating into the hates that has grown
Rape of the kid with a pretty face
There is death of the Rat that spoke a trace.
Destruction is heard smoke is seen
Deprived manhood now comes out mean
Hot summer day turns into night
Talks go on for what is right
A city of numbers eases in with the cool
Looking to the leaders for what to do
When like a mist the gas appears
Bringing forth those curtain fears
Dignity leaves when you fall to your knees
Yet pride keeps you from saying please
You fight with hate it is all you own
But hate needs food and hunger has grown
The battle is over and no one won

The fight for manhood is never done
Hot summer day with all the heat
Angry souls and high walls meet

I think about going to prisons today in 2019 and giving sermons on how best to do time. It was like I had all the answers on kicking back and just flowing with what had to be done. I was a conformist I was able to accept conditions to make the best out of the worst. I made the most of a bad situation. I went to prison because I had no focus; I had two main ingredients young & stupid. I had a seventh-grade education and I carried around my Bronx attitude like it was going to get me somewhere.

I do not recommend robbing a bank but for me it was the best thing that could have happened to me. It was like I grew up when I first entered the prison. Like my attitude took a 100% turn around.

Before I left prison, I had taken my seventh-grade education to finishing high school and going on to collage to get my AA degree. I picked up writing skills, but the most important lesson I was to learn was the value of freedom, and until you lose it, you don't know what you had. Most take it for granted.

There are people that cannot be conformed. They are set in the ways and no matter the reality they will not change. They have a pride that drives them and keeps them going. In a way I admire them but pride a form of ego cannot exist when you're locked up, surrounded by bars and walls, and rules that need to be adjusted to. You must bend or you will break.

On the other end of the spectrum was a guy named John Peiora. John was the meanest and toughest man I ever knew. He was Steven Seagal and Bruce Lee in one body. He grew up in Philippines, his dad being in the service and from the age of four until he was seventeen. He had learned every form of Martial Arts that existed. John had killed man in a bar fight and because his hands were licensed like a firearm, as lethal weapon, he was given ten years in prison for manslaughter. John Peoria was really a mellow type of guy, but he was set in his ways, he hated to be given orders, but ask him and he would comply.

John also hated bullies and in prison there are wall to wall bullies, people who prey on the weak. They take advantage of the young inmates who are scared shitless, who do not stand up for their self. Bullies see gentle or kindness as weakness and the punks sweep in on this type of person.

When you see a movie and one guy comes up against three big inmates and that one guy takes all three of them out, in less than five seconds, to where the punks are on the ground in pain, well mostly that is fiction. Yet I have seen with my own eyes John Peoria take down three guys who were bulling a young inmate.

Another thing about John was do not start anything with him, he would finish it fast. Sometimes I think prison is like the old west and when word got out who was the fastest gun in the West there was always someone who wanted to prove he was better. John did not go looking for trouble, but it always seemed to find him, and he was also the one that finished it. He was in many fights; I only saw one other besides the one when he took out those three guys, and not one time did anyone ever get a hand on him or was he ever hit, he was just that good.

John and I were friends (a good friend to have) we played handball, worked out on the weight pile together, and played some dominoes. He liked to listen to my poems, and I think they helped to ease him of some kind of inner pain he had to live with. I talk like we spent lots of time together but most of John's time was spend in solitary confinement for getting in fights. It didn't matter if it was inmate or prison guard, if you got in John's face he did not know how to back off, his instinct was to attack.

I had received forty years to begin with and was out in four years. John got ten years and when he served nine years eleven months and six days, he was let back into population to do his twenty-four more days. He served his whole ten years to the minute.

And that is the difference of being able to conform which I did to the fullest. While John was a lion and never learned that when caged you are no longer a lion. Well don't tell John that. John spent a year in the hole once for knocking out an asshole prison guard once. He became a hero to many inmates who all hated this guard.

Prison guards were respected to the sense they had a job to do, and inmates understood that. But some guards were just power hungry, and they go out of their way to make it tougher on the inmates.

Here is an example that happened to me personally that can show how petty guards can be. A friend and I were playing coin ball, a stupid game that could only be made up in prison where you have plenty of time to spare. We had a penny and we placed it between us, we would stand about 4 feet on each side of each other and we would throw a ball at the penny and if you hit it, you got a point, if you turned the penny over you got three points. The game was going on for about ten minutes and to show how boring prison can be sometimes there were about six or seven inmates watching this stupid game. All of a sudden one of those asshole guards pushes himself between the inmates and reaches down and takes the penny, saying. "This is contraband, you're lucky I don't write you up" and he walks away with our penny.

This pisses me off and I start to walk towards the guard, one of my buddies' stops me and says to me. "It's not worth it, this guard will write you up for nothing."

"I know. I just want to tell him something."

"Ok, but be careful."

"Excuse me!" I say as the guard turns around. "Yeah, what do want?" he snaps back.

"I was wondering if you ever read the comics in the paper."

"Huh, what are you talking about?" as he shakes his head not knowing what I want. No inmates ever find the time or wish to talk to him, and he is fine with that.

"Do you ever read the funnies in the paper?" I ask again. "Yeah, I do sometimes, what about it?"

"How about Peanuts have you read it before?" I ask.

"Yeah, I kind of like it, it's cute sometimes." The guard responds like we are having a conversation, something he's not use to with an inmate. I continue.

"I was reading one yesterday and Linus was playing with Lucy's toys when Lucy being the kind of mean girl she is, snatches all the toys from Linus and throw's him a rubber band and says. 'Here play with this.' Linus is a mellow dude who knows how to make the best from the worst and begins to have a blast with the rubber band. 'Wahoo and Yippy' he is saying as he stretches the rubber band every which way. Lucy comes over and grabs the rubber band from Linus and yells. 'I didn't mean for you to have fun with the rubber band and walks away."

At first the guard cracked a smile until he realized what I just did. His face wrinkles up and he cracks, "Are you referring to me taking your penny?"

"No sir. Just wanted to tell you the joke. Have a nice day," and I walked away.

John and I play hand ball the next day and he asks if I wrote any more poems. I forgot which one I read him, but it was something to do with "existing", he relates but tells me that there is more to life than just existing. I try to explain that to exist in the future sometimes you got to pay the price today. He does not comprehend as it must be his way 100% of the time all the time for him to keep his identity. He is so set in his ways there is no way to get through.

It's two days later, with only three weeks to go before John will be a free man. He is coming back from chow when he stops to talk to another inmate, which is against the rules as you are supposed to go right to your cell for a count they do after chow. They want to make sure no one escaped during dinner. There is guard who stands inside a cage and controls all the cells and who do you think was the guard on duty this night? Yes, it is the Penny Snatcher, a handle we put on this guard after the penny incident.

John is still talking to his friend when the Penny Snatcher yells out "Peiora, get in your cell!" John turns to the guard and nods as he holds up one finger, like just a second." The Penny

Snatcher then slams all the cells closed, gets out of his cage and heads towards John. We already know this guard is an asshole and today he wants to prove something to everyone. No doubt he knows that John is about to be set free and here was the Penny Snatcher's chance to show that he is a big shot. He knows John will do nothing to jeopardize his upcoming freedom.

"When I tell you to lock up, you don't hold up a finger to me, you just do as I say and you do it right then, do you understand?" Penny Snatcher yells so all can hear.

John holds his cool and says. "Sorry, just open my cell please." it should have ended there.

"Don't play that tough guy shit with me Peiora, you don't scare me!" Penny Snatcher says in a sarcastic voice.

"I am not sir, I just want to get in my cell. Will you unlock it for me please?" This whole story is all hearsay I got from the inmates, but I was told John was real patient with Penny Snatcher, but Penny Snatcher just kept pushing John.

"Do you think you're a tough guy, do you think you scare me, maybe you scare everyone else around here, but you don't scare me."

"Open my fucking cell and do it now!" An inmate who saw the look in John's eyes said the look was horrifying; the guard should have done what he was told.

"Now you're in for it Peiora, threatening a guard, you're going back to… "and it was as far as Penny Snatcher got, when John with one movement ripped Penny Snatcher's eye right out of its socket. I did not see this, but someone said the eye was hanging down with some kind of cord attached to it.

Penny Snatcher retired and was never seen inside the walls again. John Peiora received ten more years after being found guilty of first-degree assault causing disfigurement. It was more like a life sentence to John who would now become much more incorrigible; he would never see freedom again. One thing I will say about John he never stopped being a lion.

And I, the lamb, chose to write what I consider my favorite poem.

What's Behind the Words?

"YOURS TO CHOOSE"

Be timid, don't fight, and take shit not right,

For the lamb sheds its wool to clothe

Kiss ass buy time, look ahead not behind,

For what tomorrow brings you mold

The Lion can't survive inside a cage

For trapped he is no longer king

But never learning to give up its rage

Means never hearing freedom sing.

The man plays with cards stacked

If you gamble, you have to lose

You're alone, and their game is backed

The Lion or the Lamb, it is yours to choose

Be wise, not quick

Be smart not slick

For the lamb will again have his wool.

I wrote the next poem my first Thanksgiving in prison knowing it was not going to be my last. I met a fellow prisoner yesterday that has been here for seventeen years and may stay here for the rest of his life. He killed a cop in the course of a robbery. He was on death row for two years until they stopped the death penalty. He had gotten out two years earlier on work release, only to pull off more robberies.

Some people would say that is where he belongs in prison and I don't argue the point, but he is one of those inmates that has become institutionalized, who has no chance on the outside. The world had changed too much for them to fit in. They become creatures of habit or systemized. They make the bells that ring throughout the day become part of their brain cells telling them when to eat, when to go to work, when to go the yard, when to go to bed. I knew I was not part of this group as the bell never stopped driving me crazy, I never got used to the bells.

There are so many different types of people here and I am just one of them. Really, am I?

"FOR WHAT, I SAY"

Many different people, many different places,

Many different forms, many different races.

All lonely all searching for their place in life

Many leaving behind children and a wife

For what, for what I say, what's it all for

They had all they needed but then wanted more

Most smart, some dumb, some angry, some fun

Most hurt, some cry, most live, some die.

For what, for what I say, is it their own will?

Is it the money, or the seeking of a thrill?

The answer the reason, the purpose of it all

I can't put my finger on yet it seems so small.

Then I ask myself, for one the different people are me.

For what, for what is say, why couldn't I stay free?

Karma, even if you deny it, it won't matter, it exists. There is a balance and I truly believe most people get what they got coming, good or bad, dues will be paid. The more you give in life the more you will get, it works the other way also.
Hence= Karma.

"ACCOUNTS RECEIVBLE"

Borrowing from the bank of life, we have all made the loan.

It comes when we are in need, giving is the only payback known.

Some continue to borrow without too much thought, making loans interest due

Payment is never forgot, every day will bring you a certain clue.

The conscience receives the bill there is no bankruptcy in giving

Leaving it all to your will and how you choose to do your living.

Well this lad borrowed. To full extent, kept putting payment off till tomorrow

Giving felt cheated of rent, tipping the scales to sorrow.

What comes around, goes around, the bank of life keeps the books.

For what I owe, I now pay. Why not? It is my debt.

It is now August 13th, nope the 14th 2.30 am, just got back from playing poker, won a $800 pot if you include the $200, I got for making the high hand, four 7s plus the pot of $600.

Nice timing. Oh well on with the story; I was going through some ugly times within myself and questioning how my life had come to where it was. How could I have been so stupid? As the last poem I wrote, this is also a down poem, I had not yet to learn acceptance. I try to look back to envision my conditions and it is like ten lifetimes ago, all I can do is quote my journal. And the poem will explain where my head was...

"PAYBACK"

Oh, isn't life great when everything is going fine

How life rolls along when you're having a good time

No time to think of bad, I took for granted the way I feel

But the trip is over and Hell becomes what is real

I just can't imagine how this could be happening to me

How could I jeopardize all I loved, especially being free?

Now it tears inside me, I feel close to hate

I find it hard to believe that this was my fate

Oh sure I done wrong and sure I should pay

But isn't it enough for just the pain I feel today

Nope for what I did one day, I got to pay back 2000 more

Humility will be plentiful and there are sorrows galore

So eat your heart Sucker, isn't payback a bitch

You never knew when you were free, it was then you were rich.

Prison can be the ugliest place on earth, you see things that you want or wish you could change, but you are powerless, you can't put yourself in harm's way to protect a young kid who is being butchered by evil people. Not literally but his soul is.

I was in the yard with my chess game looking for anyone who wanted to play for a few packs of smokes, I liked my odds, and I played a good game of chess. As I walked around the track I looked over at the wall and there leaning against it was a new young inmate who was no doubt was crying but was hiding it with his head between his knees. He was like many of young inmates who were scared to death when they entered prison. Young stupid kids sent to this hell hole for charges like DUI, Burglary, many of them are here for selling pot which in 1977 was big no-no. Bottom line they did not deserve to be thrown into a lion's pit.

Prison has no shortage of predators and they swoop in on these kids and scare them, beat them up a little to make them their slave. And like wolf's devourer a carcass they turn these kids into zombies. Sexual slaves, money sent from home, make my bed slave, anything that devours the young kid's soul and self-respect.

I walked over to the kid who had no friends and asked him if he would like to play a game of chess. He looked up at me with his watery eyes, wiped them with his sleeve and had a look like, what the hell do you want from me.

"Yeah, I have no one to play with and you didn't look to busy, so I thought I ask you if you want to have a game of chess?" I hoped I came across like I didn't want anything from him but to have a game of chess. I saw what looked like light enter this kid, like it was the first kind thing said to him since he entered the walls.

"Yes, I like chess, really you want to play a game?" he looked right into my eyes like he was looking for some kind of condition; a price to pay for what he saw was my kindness.

I put my back against the wall and slid down it, placing the chess board between us. "I don't carry this game around for my health. Great let's have a game." I poured the pieces out of the bag and grabbed two pawns, did a shuffle and put my hand out for him to choose what color he would be. He let out a breath, a sigh of comfort and a smile came to his face as he picked a hand.

His name was Kenny and he received three years for five pounds of weed he was busted with. He also had a loaded gun on his person which brought about the prison sentence. He was married less than a year against both of their parent's wishes, but young love is pretty powerful and they didn't care, they would make it on their own. But love and reality have different understandings. And especially when his wife came down with some health issues and could not afford doctors or medicine. He did what he had to do.

I wrote this poem that night and decided after it was over that I was going to do something to help Kenny out, I liked the kid. I had some pull around the prison I was going to use it. I will continue with the story after the poem.

"THE DAY LOVE DIED"

Young in life, heart full of love with only lessons of
years missing

They would go with their hearts just knowing life has
its blessings

Wedding bells rang, no need to postpone

Love would supply even if parents condone.

If only life was as easy as love, if needs came from the heart, if harmony could take away hunger, if reality could make love smart, if 'if' could pay the rent.

Doctors can't spend love, its money they crave

She was sick, so it made him brave

Gun in shaking hand thinking love protects

Too soft to demand, now society collects.

The day love died.

Kenny was not much of a chess player, but he enjoyed the stress-free time he had until a punk convict I know as Roach walked over to us. I saw Kenny tense up.

"Hey Kenny, good buddy, how about you and me go for a walk?" Roach said in a mean tone. I knew he wanted Kenny for some sex but what he just did was way out of line. First off, he may disrespect Kenny, but what he just did was disrespect me. In this environment respect was everything, you can't lose it for a second or you could lose it forever.

I slowly got up looking right at Roach who I saw show unease, I knew he was a punk, and punks lack balls. He stood over 6ft tall and had 60 pounds over my 5ft. 5in. 160- pound frame, he was a punk. I also knew he had seen me running with my clique and us all working out in the weight pile and many knew John Peoria was a friend of mine, but at this point it was me and this punk, I got right in Roach's face.

"What the fuck you think you're doing; do you see me playing chess with this kid?"

"I got some business with the guy; didn't think you would mind!" His voice no longer had a mean tone.

"Get the fuck out of here!" I said in my hard ass voice. And turned my back on him and made like I was going to sit back down.

"Ok, you don't have get so pissed!" was all he got out and I turned back around and moved toward him. He did as I hoped and backed up.

"Get the fuck out of here, now"

"Ok, I'm leaving" Roach said at the same time he was walking away.

I sat back down and asked Kenny if he had moved yet, I saw the admiration. "How did you do that? That guy is twice your size. I mean who are you, why did you pick me to play chess with, I mean I don't understand what just happened?" Kenny ended his questions, just as the 5-minute bell rang to clear the yard. I grabbed the bag and started putting the chess pieces away without answering any of Kenny's questions.

"Your game will get better, let's play again tomorrow. This is a good spot see you then, by the way who has you working for him?" I asked as I folded the chess board, I tried to show the kid some slack and not ask him who was pimping him off.

"What do you mean?" was what came out of his mouth.

"Kenny, I been here long enough to know what you are going through, I don't know why, but I am going to try to help you, but you always got to play straight with me, never bullshit me, never. Now once again, who's stable are you in?" I was blunter this time.

"Kyle Henry's crew," he whispered out as he looked down in some kind of shame.

"Ok, see you tomorrow, right?" and we headed into the cell blocks.

The above story and my tough guy attitude ends there as the solution to freeing Kenny had narrowed down to like all things in life, Money and Politics. I knew Kyle Henry was part of the Aryan Brotherhood and they are more about greed then brotherhood.

I managed a softball team with nothing but murders on it and I had George playing the outfield. He had a great arm, hit over 400, and was in command of the Gang Aryan Brotherhood. He was also into me for over twenty cartons of smokes which he had lost in the football pool I had implemented.

George had come to softball practice like he did five times a week along with fifteen other players on my team, you miss practice, and you don't play in the next game. I have to admit I was a tough coach and, but it showed as we won 90% of our games, it also helped me in the respect department. I pulled George to the side. This is how the conversation went.

"Hey George, you have young kid in your stable named Kenny?"

"Yeah!" George snapped back in surprise never knowing I was into sex with men. "Why, you want some action?"

"Come on, you know me better than that George." I had come up with a story as I did not want to show weakness as my reason of just wanting to help someone out. In prison kindness is taken for weakness. "He is my wife's cousin and my family asked me to look over him."

"Wow Ron, how come I am just hearing about this now, the kid has been in my stable since he got here two months ago. He is good too; I mean he is a cash cow, what do you want from me?" I knew he knew what I was going to ask him, or he would not have said anything about Kenny being a cash cow, he was already advertising for what I was going to ask him.

"Cut the kid loose, George, what do you think I want?

"You are a funny guy Ron, you pop off a demand to me like you're talking to anyone and I admire that, you throw your little self-authority around, like you're a King or the meanest mother fucker who ever lived. We all take it, not only that we love you for it. Yeah, I can help you out, but business is business, it's going to cost you!"

"Fine George, tell me what it is going to take and while you at it, throw in protection on the kid, I don't want nothing to happen to him." It proved to be wise insurance for Kenny when he was approached by Roach, and Kenny told him he doesn't have to do that no more and Roach slapped him, only for Roach to end up in the hospital with broken ribs and broken nose.

I ended up forgiving George of his debt to me and added a 100-carton credit he could use in the future, or I should say lose in the future, George was a terrible gambler. So, in reality it cost me nothing to save a young kid, who I feel was on the verge of suicide. Did I feel like a hero, I don't know Kenny thought so and showed when he was let out of prison after six months. Prison had an overcrowding issue at the time, what am I saying, it is now forty years later, and prison has a worst overcrowding issue, anyway, sorry sometimes my mind wonders and I forget what I am doing or writing when my mind takes over to what it is thinking right that moment.

In the six months Kenny remained at O.S.P. he had learned a trade he used to get a job when he got out. Kenny wrote me for two years until I got out, I would receive photos of his young wife and after a year, photos of their new baby girl. I never thought about any of this when I decided to help him out, but it did inspire a poem that I wrote when I heard about his new baby.

"SOMETIMES"

Who knows why you do some things just because you can

You do it by impose not knowing how it could end

You don't think of consequences or trouble it could be

Sometimes you do stuff because that's just me.

Now it is August 15th, 2019, 3:11 am the day before my birthday, I am going to be 71 years old. How I made it this far is a true wonder. Any other country would have assassinated me by now. Or the lifestyle I live, the food that I eat, and the crazy hours I sleep should have killed me by now. No, I am like a Timex, I just keep on ticking. Each day I wake, I say thanks because I am sure I am on borrowed time.

I just got home from the Muckleshoot Indian Casino where I go most days to play poker. Today was a winning day, not much but after being stuck over $500 and end up winning $200, well it was $700 turn around. Poker has become my life since I retired, trouble is I've been retired, it seems, my whole life.

I am a contented man; in fact, I am perfectly content. Is it my attitude? It could be maybe, but life is good to me, we own a house, three cars, not fancy ones, but the best cars ever invented; paid off cars. All my children are healthy. Money is nothing great but as long as Valarie keeps on working making her 60K a year, along with my social security, and I keep on winning the 20K that I have average over the last 12 years, we will survive.

I am a little worried; no, I am really worried about Valarie with her Rheumatoid arthritis and the pain she hides from me. It just does not seem fair as she has lived an exemplarily healthy life. She never smoked or did drugs, and she has been a vegetarian most of her life. It just makes no sense. She tries not to complain but when she comes to me to button her blouse or to open a can or bottle because she has lost use of her fingers in those capacities, I know how much she is hurting. Still, she goes to work every day; she's been working from home the last two years of her twelve years with Alaska Airlines. She needs to do a lot typing and she does it with her hands the way they are, she is remarkable. She is my hero is all I can say and that she has been my blessing for 37 years now.

She is also very Christian; she doesn't talk about it she just does it. She gives within her heart into so many different ways. She is a big supporter of the military and has worked with Home Front an organization the helps soldiers in need for twelve years. Anyway, she is just a good person. God loves her so much and I get the overflow of God's love for her; when I screw up God just says, "Oh that is Valerie's husband just let it slide."

I think there is more praying at the poker tables than there is in church, but God doesn't play poker and could care less when a poker player prays for the magic card to come under their breath. When the card does not come, they now blame him, with a God damn it. Sorry folks, you lost again, this time is for higher stakes.

I used those prayers when I was in my last hand, with my last bit of money, not only mine but the money I borrowed from a loan shark and I lost. My prayers were answered by the loan shark after I put him off for payment to long, handing me a gun saying. "You get us our money, don't care how, you just get it and it better be soon."

Which brings me back to prison and prayers and God. Any excuse that can justify what is happening in life, but I guess it is not just prison people who have used God as an escape or excuse for situations, usually when you are in need or want. Just ask God, and if your prayer is not answered then you can blame God. They use God as a game. Did I just did say they when I really meant me.

"TIME TO WIN"

So hard to follow, so easy to stray, the confusion I find trying to be your way

To give you praise for disappointments too, for I know all things come from your will.

It is so hard when I can't understand, the purpose behind when you make a demand

But praise you ask so it will be praise that I give, for I now know it is for your spirit I live.

Just one thing from you I would like to ask, as you say in prayer you perform all tasks

I pray you will answer for I ask not in greed, nor for what I want, but what I need

Oh Lord, my God, My Savior power of all, I know I have wronged many so the ask is not small

What I ask my Father is to take away all my sin, for I am tired of losing it's time to win.

In order to do time, you must shake away any thoughts of the free world on the other side of the wall. Inside, becomes your world and you must always try to make the most of the world you are in. That works on most things right up to the first thought of your little 8-year boy who is trapped in the real world waiting for his dad to come get him.

I think of Shane constantly and it is the only time I cry. I think of when he was two years old laying next to his dead mother

---

Rosy for almost two days before she was discovered. I think of him living with his mother dead and his father in prison.

Rosy was my first love, you know the love that you use as a guideline the rest of your life, the love you never forget, especially when they die. The love gets tattooed into your soul. Rosy was sixteen when I married her, I was nineteen. No, she was not pregnant at the time, but she had a hard life and a perverted father with a half-crazy mother and they were all happy to have her move out and marry me. We were married July 24th, 1967 in Reno Nevada. The first of three marriages in Reno, the preacher said after my third marriage if I came back again, he would give me a group rate, but I am getting ahead of myself again.

When we got married, I was working for Boeing, what I consider the only real job I have had in my life. It was a great paying job, and I was making $3.04 an hour. I was driving a brand new 1967 Mustang fast-back which I bought for $2900, and I had a $90 a month payment. Our 1-bedroom apartment was only $65 a month. We were living the young married couple's dream. But nothing lasts forever and when I was caught sleeping on the job and fired, the dream kind of ended and I became a hustler which introduced me to other hustlers until I ended up in the Carnival. Shane was born October 4th, 1969, and his first two years was without a dad as I was always on the road.

When Rosy died I was on the road in the Carnival it was 1972; I was having the time of my life. I was making more money than I ever had because they had a great pay plan for a business that dealt only in cash, and no one but you knew how much you took in. The pay was 50% of what I took in and 100% of what I could steal. It was not unusual for me to have over a $1000 in my pocket for one day, this was in the early 70s, and I lived like a millionaire. There was a different town every week and a different woman every night. I am sure you have heard of groupies in bands, well you would be surprised what a young lady will do for a Teddy Bear. I worked the rip-off games that let a person win when you wanted them to, and impossible for the suckers to win when you didn't want them to. As you can see, I wasn't a very nice guy when I was twenty-two years old. You the reader, are probably wondering what kind of game I controlled that I could make a sucker out of people and that no way would be able to trick me. I was really good at what I did and believe me if you have the two ingredients of money in your pocket and believe there is something for nothing, I would get you too. I had many scores for over $1000 bucks. I don't want to give away the secrets as my next book is going to be about the carnival and I will divulge the whole story in that book.

You live the lifestyle getting the best rooms, you could eat hamburger, but it was steak every night, I sent Rosy home $200 to $300 a week, I was in my Disneyland until I got the call that Rosy had died.

Rosy died of pneumonia; nobody dies of pneumonia in 1972 you get a shot of penicillin and it goes away. But not Rosy who had paranoia of hospitals from when she broke her arm and the hospital had set the arm wrong and Rosy had to go back for a painful re-break and set again. It took an act of God for her to go to the hospital to have Shane. So, when she got sick, she just thought she would ride the sickness out, it did not work, it killed her, she was only twenty years old.

I had to quit the Carnival; I had a son to raise. That is what I told myself that I was going to grow up overnight become a real man and be the best Father in the world.

I got on at a state-run program that paid me to go to school. Up until this point in my life I only had a seventh-grade education, and the state was going to pay for schooling.

They offered me $300 a month to live while I attended trade school. So, I took the program and decided I was going to be an accountant.

I went to Bates Vocational School in Tacoma and in no time at all I met the cutest little lady by the name of Patti Sage. I guess I swept her off her feet and it wasn't long before we were making love. I liked Patti, but that was all, Rosy had been dead less than six months. When she said she was pregnant and wanted me to marry her, I felt it was what I had to do. Besides, she would be a great baby-sitter for Shane.

Off to Reno for marriage number two. It was a terrible honeymoon, she was on her period and the romance was pathetic. I felt I made a mistake and was tricked into marriage. We came home and Patti, un-like Rosy who had morning sickness the first month of her pregnancy, had none of this. I finally just came out and asked, "You're not really pregnant, are you?"

She looked at me with them beautiful brown eyes and said "No." so after 4 days I was married no more.

I quit the school one morning asking myself, what the hell was I doing, I don't want to be an accountant, and I quit. But years later I was thankful for what I had learned in accounting, as it came in handy in the businesses I venture into. You see in life nothing should ever be wasted we are what we are through experience; It won't be the last time you see me use that phase.

The day I quit school I went on an LSD trip and I wrote the following. So, you will be in the same thought about this poem. "HUH"

"FLOWING"

Look around, think profound, all of the sounds that are going around.

Listen from deep within are the secrets, the longed for answers lives within

Sadness with my head never does meet. Happy is the cry I squeak

Looking and searching for unknown, yet the party is a blast, the hurt is comfort and sorrow is masked.

Dying expressions never game, overlapping fears just the same.

Memories can't drive tomorrow's ship sailing into the sunset of rainbows

Unforgotten breeze blowing waste, pictures of yesterday I taste.

What's Behind the Words?

Crying but tears never show from yesterday sadness flows.

*A feeble attempt to a swoon degree of forever trying to
end a spree*

*Heights never reached in human mind with a hunger to speak
inner sights*

*Long lasted visions into wastefulness claiming all that is not
yet forgotten*

*Speak unto your lost mighty man; shed no greedy costs
if you can*

Tell me truth oh heavenly beast, words full of wisdom uphold

Waiting and yearning at last paid, like a bright light it shone

Coming home to true reward, Let it be, let it be.

Now it is August 19th, 2019, I haven't written for a couple of days. The thought of me going back to prison is bringing back so many thoughts. I try to portray that while I was in prison, I was having the time of my life, but truth be told, I hated it and I counted each day as a day closer to freedom.

Freedom, ahh man, such a strong word, how you truly know its meaning when you no longer have it. And me who has always been so care free, doing what I wanted most of my life, finding out I have lost that due to confinement, well I hated being locked up. I played the games with my mind that I had to while I was there, but even now forty years later, I get chills thinking about me locked up.

So, you know what? Silly question, how would you know what, I am the one writing, but I am going to escape from prison for a while and go to another portion of my life, like sixteen years later as I am reading my Journal from 1998-1999.

Someone asked me if I am writing my life story. I never thought of it that way, my first thought was to find an interesting way to publish my poems. But as I read back, and see how it is all coming together, I am writing my life's story, and I am throwing in a mixture of poems.

And why not, it is not like this is going to be a blockbuster, or make me any kind of money, who the hell cares about some unknown dude they never met and what his life story is.

So, to my friends, my family, for hopefully generations to come I write this for you, in hopes that within the writing there are some lessons. I mean I have sold over 600 copies of "Rest Stop", I don't have that many friends and family, so there is some kind of market out there. But mostly I envision my grandkids looking at my stories and my ego sees them going "Wow, grandpa, was a cool dude; he sure had an interesting life, wish I got to meet him!"

Yes, I feel I am an individual, as we all are, but there is only one of me and I do feel like I am a cool dude and have had an interesting life. So on with the story.

March 1998.

Valarie and I went on a Mexican cruise and we had a blast. But I believe in fate, and that things don't just happen, there is a reason for things to come together.

To be on a cruise and run into someone you know, who you worked with in the past, well, what are the chances? That is an example of the fate I am talking about. His name was Steve Belnap and together we did consulting work five years earlier for my Brother Ed's motorcycle consulting business. Steve and I worked at the same locations in different parts of the country together. We shared a room, dinners, and many conversations and had become good friends. We both went separate ways when our tour was done, and it had been 5 years since I had seen him.

Steve was just starting a business in Utah that dealt with remodeling homes and he told me he needed a good Sales Manager. He knew of my sales ability and offered me the position. Since I had nothing really planned for a job after the cruise, I jumped at the chance for us to work together again.

"Sounds good Bro, but shit I don't know anything about remodeling!" I said to Steve who came back with the perfect answer.

"I don't need you to hammer nails; I need your sales ability." I was in and ready to head to Utah as soon as the cruise was over. I was about to try something I had never done before, but then life is all about our experiences.

"INSPIRED"

A new adventure from an old experience, a mixture of new and old. Should equal success

An opportunity from becoming mature can be turned into excellence

The desire to do what needs to be done, the ambition to do it.

The should of, could of, would of are here, now this minute.

Acceptance of hard work, acceptance of integrity, the desire to excel

The desire to forget the bad and move on to the good.

Fresh, brand new start, reborn, it's my ball, the touchdown is in view.

The sights are refreshing and achievable; it is in your hands to do.

To accomplish, to achieve, you have all the tools, now build your castle.

You can see by this poem that this new venture I am about to pursue was going to get all my heart. I was all gung-ho. But like many times in my life, I would envision all the good and not see all that was about to take place in order to pursue this new quest.

One of the things I picked up from my dad, who was also a dreamer and had tried countless ventures of his own, he was always making a million before he made his first dollar.

I didn't think about having to leave my family while I was in Utah, the living conditions I would need, or transportation to get around. No, all I saw was a new adventure and the possibility of making $1000's of dollars.

"HERE FOR A REASON"

So it is in the stars, maybe up in Mars.

The pearly gate or perhaps fate

But you're here for a reason

Take the good and the bad, the happy and the sad

There is no sorrow for a future tomorrow

You're here for a reason

There is money to earn, lessons to learn.

The visions are bright as I write tonight

I'm here for a reason

And yes it is lonely for family only

I am doing as I should for the long run good

And remember, I am here for a reason.

It doesn't take long to realize that maybe I made the wrong discussion. Steve Belnap's ego is bigger than mine. I had to learn that when I came up with an idea I wanted to implement, I had to make it look like Steve's idea in order for him to approve it. I was not given the free hand I was promised, but I am a master at manipulation.

I have moved into a boarding house with one room, sharing a bathroom, fridge, and microwave. I begin to see difference between the money I was told I could make and what I am actually making. I mean what I am making here I could be making at home and being with my family without all the changes I am going through. I still need to pay all the expenses in Washington and now the expenses here in Utah. I am the type of guy that once negative slips in, it is hard to come back out.

"NO PAIN, NOTHING GAINED"

Life's decisions change so fast, highs of yesterday don't seem to last

Attitude gives way to change; ego plays a game so strange

What's Behind the Words?

Sights of basics come in view; you go and grab what you have to do.

Nothing lost or nothing gained, wasn't hard I felt no pain

Life goes on with lessons learned, didn't gain too much but wasn't burned

Not leaving with my tail between my legs, I wrote the script, I went on stage

I played a role an image planted, had not received what I was granted

So no complaints the days went by, not so sure that I even tried

Another experience under my belt, doesn't always work out to how I felt.

So, I come home, and I go to work for my old friend Seymour Flop, not his real name but one he picked up playing poker because he was known to see more flops then all the other players. He is a great guy and always has my back if I am in need.

He owns Carz-4-U on South Tacoma way. He lets me come in when I want, gives me a demo and days off when I want and money if I need it. In the car business this is called the Three Ds. A Draw, a Demo and a Day Off. I am what they call a prima-donna. Why may you ask? Well, I am the best salesman around, I produce sales, money reduce inventory and get the most out of deal, or otherwise I am a prima-donna. Besides me and Seymore are about as tight of friends as you can have between an owner and a salesman.

I was right about leaving Utah and being able to make as much money as I could there, right here at home, with my family to go home to every night. In fact, I am hungry, broke and on fire on the sales floor and I make $10,000 my first month back, and Seymore knows it there is nothing better than a hungry salesman, so he gets out my way and I take care of business.

Some people may wonder what my secret is, how am I always the top salesman, well I am going to let you in on my secret. I have sold many different products and always did well because of these 2 steps:

#1. Make it easy for the customer to buy.

#2. Make the customer feel like a winner.

You accomplish those two things and no matter the product, you will get the sale.

Within a couple of months I am back on my feet. Valarie is happy, the kids are happy, bills are paid, and I love going to work. That alone is a win, if I enjoy what I am doing I even get better at what I do. Yep, I am a made man.

"REAL MADE MAN"

Surprises in life are yet to be seen

There are ups and downs and in-betweens

With hidden doors full of history

All in disguise and full of mystery

There are bends and curves and unknown turns

A bunch of smooth rides a few gentle burns

And after the rides are over and out

You learn to reject all of the doubt

Views come of contentment and peace

The inner feelings can be released

Somehow this hatches a real made man

A guy who always knew that he can

To shed the cocoon that made him slack

That had a way of holding him back

He metamorphosized into his true form

Atlas singing his well-written song

Out will sprout the real inner self

Bringing with it, contentment, happiness, and wealth

So just cruise along you are doing your time,

July 24, 1998

I don't understand me! Why I want to quit a job where I am making over $5,000 a month. Is it I get bored, is it I have broken all the records, have gotten all the spiffs? Have I lost the challenge, is not my family happy, and haven't you gotten out of debt because of this job? Not even five months, yet it is longer than I ever stayed at a car lot before.

I can't blame it on poker this time. Before I would only work long enough to get my stake, then kick ass in poker and give up my job until I went broke. Then have no problem getting hired until the cycle would start again.

No, this time there is a great reason to quit, so enter the life of Ron Lemco, Real World Selling. Yes, I am quitting because I am starting my own business. Maybe I should say we are starting our own business, Valarie and I. We make a great team. We have worked alongside each other many times, she understands me after 17 years together, and she is my partner in so many ways.

Hard to understand as we are totally different; other than the kids and when we work together, we are complete opposites. Val, doesn't smoke, do drugs, she is a vegetarian, stays away from sweets, could care less about poker other then maybe hate it for the times I would come home broke, or lose the rent money. Yet she would console me. She knew I would bounce back as I always do and within a few days I would be working again, and stay until I made a big score at the poker tables, or take off a big tournament for $10,000 to $15,000, it wouldn't be the first time. She accepted it; she accepts me and all my downfalls. She is a computer wizard compared to me the computer dummy. My sexual appetite is way beyond hers, yet in seventeen years she has never said no, she has said "Just don't wake me up!" and I accept that, but mostly we click well together.

Now my new idea, Real World Selling, is about all I know about salesmanship. I was a consultant in my Brother Ed's business in the motorcycle industry for 4 years. Money was fantastic, $1500 a day plus expenses, but I got burned out, living out of a suitcase and being away from the family for weeks at a time.

There are 100 times more car lots then there are Motorcycle dealerships. For thirty years I have been a top selling salesman, I know my shit when it comes to sales. Why not go to dealerships and train their salespeople over again. I know salesman and many of them burn out or lose their edge. They become conditioned and try to short cut sales procedures, they have forgotten the basics. I bring them back to basics; re-teach the seven steps of car sales. #1 the greeting, #2 the probe, #3 the demo, #4 get them inside the office, #5 the write up, #6 the close, #7 the delivery. That folks are the basics and so many salespeople try to by-pass steps and forget that all seven steps are needed. I come into the dealership and re-hash and teach each step again.

The second part of the business of Real World Selling is the employment agency. I sell trained young salesman who will know the seven steps and are hungry to show their skills, and dealerships will pay me $1000 for a fully trained salesperson. These new kids, we call them green peas in the industry, will be able to take a customer from the greeting all the way to the close. I can train a class of ten salespeople in six days, which could mean $10,000 a week. There is a need for this agency as salespeople are always in demand. Anyway, that is Real World Selling, and I am all pumped up and ready to go. Valarie has put together 100 letters we wrote together, got the addresses of dealerships, and we are ready to go.

"THE TEAM"

We've been here before, haven't we, you and I with a vision

With bright lights ahead with sights of worries none.

We have proven it before, haven't we, you and I are a team

*Work doesn't scare us, does it? Any hours together
bring results*

*We know about ends that have brought failure, you and I have
learned our lessons*

We know that without failure there is no success,

And we have grown, we have really grown.

*We have paid our dues, haven't we, you and I we
deserve a break.*

*Yet it hasn't been bad, has it, we have laughed a lot
together anyway*

*We have just a few hills ahead, and then there comes
the coasting*

*Until we just roll along, doing what we are good at, as we
are the team.*

August 23, 2019 2:00am

I just got home from the Muckleshoot Poker Room. Where I flopped three 5s another guy flopped three 3s and a guy with a J-6 of clubs called both our all-ins, it was about a $800 pot. The flop is 345 with two clubs, and sure enough a 2 on the turn, no pair on the river, the J-6 takes the pot down with a straight. And you know what I say, "That's poker".

So, it has been a few days since I wrote, just didn't have the feel. I can't fall asleep until 6 am because I stay in bed until 3pm. So where was I a few days ago, oh yeah? I quit my job to start Real World Selling.

August 11, 1998.

The concept I have is right on, I am dealing in a win-win product. I hire kids who have no job; I teach them the basics of car sales, they have a career, win-win.

There are car lots looking for salespeople. I provide trained salespeople for a $500 fee (I lowered my original price of $1000). The car lot wins, I win, and everybody wins.

To date I have put $2200 into the business, the cost of Newspaper ads (this was before the internet was popular) and the cost of renting a training room in a hotel.

I am training my 2nd class that has fourteen people in it, my first class had nine. Out of the nine in the class, six graduated because three quit when they realized sales were not for them. And it is true, sales are not for everyone. You see who has it when it is their turn to get in front of the class and role play.

Out of the six that graduated I get three placed in jobs and I am paid $1500. Two of them went to a car lot that I had no contract with and went to work for them, that really pissed me off, and I would make sure that did not happen again. And the last one decided to go back to their old job.

No car lots are interested in the in-house training, so my only source is in training and placing want-to-be salespeople. I know my future success is going to come from how good the salespeople I place do, so I make sure that those that finish the class have the seven steps down.

I am feeling pretty good it is all starting to fall into place.

"MAGIC BUS"

Hey magic bus you came and you picked me up; you led me to the drinking cups.

You gave me my ticket that I waited for years; you ease me out of ingrown fears

I had to walk a lot of miles to get to this spot, and now I get to ride on top.

It is like I received a season pass, yet it came too easy for me to grasp.

What's Behind the Words?

Real World Selling even gets better when I snap to the outside sales that are going on every weekend, somewhere. When five or six car lots get together find a venue like a mall, or a racetrack, anyplace big enough to park at least 1000 cars, the lots pitch in and flood the market with advertising.

All the ads on TV, radio, and newspaper are yelling out, the best deals ever, and the biggest inventory, whatever. The ads work the people show, so much so that it is hard for people to find a salesperson. Ha Ha, welcome aboard Real World Selling and the car lots can care less who sells their car.

I bring in a crew of trained salespeople to greet the people, all the sales we produce gets 25% of the gross profit on the sale. I pay my salesperson 15%, which pays me 10% on every sale, I and all my crew produce. I make 25% on my personal sales, but I find little time to sell as my crew is keeping me busy. Again, it becomes a win-win, as my new salespeople fall right into action and get trained in real life sales right out of the classroom. Those that do well and impress a car lot are automatically scooped up and hired and I make another $500.

"I'M BACK"

Well didn't you know all along, that one day you would sing your song

All the visions are so clear and bright and the high hopes are clean out of sight

Finding what was there all along, your past led you here so you did no wrong

It came so easy not much of a fight, maybe all along I been right

It has all been a train ride all along, when you felt weak was when you got strong

Sure there were downs that brought you fright, but your ego reengaged tonight

August 24, 2019 3:20 A.M.

I am finding myself changing the format as I continue to work on "What's Behind the Words". I think since I have accepted that I am really writing my life story, well every night why not start off on how this day went just so the reader can get a sense of how my lifestyle is. It sure is not for everybody.

Valarie and I went to the Flight Museum tonight to see and learn about Man's first adventures in space travel, all the way until they landed on the moon, yep, we beat the Russians.

Valarie gets a call from her sister saying her Dad has been rushed to the hospital, his kidneys have shut down. This is at 8:30 at night. Without hesitation Valarie checks available flights leaving tonight; there is a last one heading to Las Vegas leaving at 9:50. She has no clothes, none of her medicine, but says "Let's try to make it", we are twenty minutes from the airport. She has worked for Alaska Airlines for twelve years and knows you have to be there twenty minutes before the flight is to take off. That means we have exactly an hour do to all of the following: We must get out of the Flight Museum, five minutes to get to the car leaving fifty-five minutes. Twenty minutes to get to the airport, traffic permitting, thirty-five minutes left. Depending on security and TSA and how long the lines are she looks like she is going to make it as my lack of fear about speeding and knowing a back way, with GPS's help and getting to the airport in fifteen minutes.

I tell Val I will wait in the cell phone parking lot to I hear if she got on the flight, if not there was an 8am flight in the morning. She calls me, letting me know how helpful everyone at the airport, who knows Valarie, pushed her through all the lines and right up to the plane and she got on. Valarie is loved by many at the airport.

My daughter Destiny calls to say she got a ticket for $200 on that 8am flight and asked if I could meet her in Federal Way and bring her Valerie's medicine and some clothes at 6:15 this morning. I tell her no problem; I will be there at McDonalds at 6:15 with her Mother's stuff.

I just got off the phone with Valarie to see what she wants me to send. I think of how strong my wife is, the poor kid worked all day, we go to the Flight Museum, make the rush to the airport. She makes the two-and-a-half-hour flight, rents a car, drives the two hours to the hospital to find out her dad is not doing so good.

Jimmy Higgins is his name the kind of guy that is the backbone of this country. The reason I love this country, it surely is not the politicians, but the working-class all- American guys like Jimmy Higgins. The guy who graduates from high school, goes in the armed forces, serves his country, comes home gets married has 4 children, goes to work every day, pays taxes, votes and is flat out a great guy. Yeah, that is the kind of guy that will get a daughter to drop everything and get to him as soon as possible. A granddaughter to run to her mother's aid. And even a son-in-law that loves Jimmy like he is his dad. Yep, ladies and gentlemen that is what you call family, and I am proud to be part of the Higgins family. And that was how the day went. I have decided to quit writing for the day and do some praying for this great American dad. Talk to you all tomorrow. First a quick prayer I will write right now.

Dear Lord, I come to you this morning and ask for your help in watching over my father-in-law Jimmy Higgins. He is a good man, never did wrong to a neighbor, I know of no lies he has told, or of anything he has ever taken not belonging to him. He has always walked a straight path Lord. He is so loved Lord and so are you by all who love him, so we put our trust in you Lord to do what is best, either way Lord we know he is in your hands, but if you can heal him so we may one more time tell him that he is loved, that would be nice. In the name of the Father, Amen.

August 24, 2019 9:20pm

I slept all day after the weird night last night. I called Valarie and her dad, shows no improvement but he is breathing on his own and Jimmy being the type of guy he is, it could be all the ammunition he needs to pull through this.

I forgot to tell you last night after Valarie made the flight, I had lots on my mind and there is no better escape from reality then playing poker, and boy I ran so lucky. Played 1-3 no-limit won $300, then got called to the 3-5 no-limit and believe this after 50 years of playing I have never gone around the table winning every hand, yes, eight hands in a row. I only won $300 more as I was playing with smart players who knew to stay out of my way, and I never hooked them for much of a pot. But it was sure nice. I wondered if Jimmy was looking over my shoulder. I go home $600 to the good. Now back to the book I am supposed to be writing.

July 1998.

So, I am holding workshops every week, I have advanced my training along with getting smarter myself. I used to rent a room in the hotel/motels to hold my class at a cost of about $600 for the 7 days of training. When I am training salespeople to go to work for car lots that have their own sales meetings space, I make them an offer. When a car lot says they are interested in hiring one of my graduating students I make them the offer, that if I can use their space, they will get pick of the litter for half price, and they can sit in the meeting and see which one to pick. The plan works and I never have to rent a room again.

How does a guy take young kids, get them to attend a class, and teach them enough to have a career, a good career in 7 days? Then get a car lot to pay $500, which I am thinking about going up to $600 soon? Well simple answer of how I do it, I will have to let my Ego explain. I am the best salesperson I know, and my training is Real World Selling, what it takes to make a sale. I teach the basics, that I know when I am the line selling and not doing so good is because I am side stepping not taking the time, not following the 7 steps, short cutting.

My kids will tell you about Dad's short cuts when I was driving them somewhere it always took longer. Well, the same thing happens in sales; you need to follow the steps, do them in order, and slow down. I have 26 points or stories to tell in the 6 days of training that covers most sales encounters. I explain the philosophies of the customer and it all narrows down to after all the training is the two main points "Make it easy for the customer to buy, and make them feel like a winner," It takes the 6 days to show them how to do this.

I have given each of the 26 lessons a letter, and since there are 26 letters in the alphabet we go from A- to Z on the courses. I don't think I will bore you and go through all 26 lessons, but I will cover some so you can get a picture of the information I presented.

Lesson #B, when you quit learning, you quit growing. I teach the importance of always keeping your mind and ears open. This class will teach you the basics, but you will learn more in a few weeks of doing what you were trained to do then you learned in class. By watching what other salesman do, especially the ones getting the sales. And the most important is something I call "The Agonizing Reappraisal", when you lose a sale and reappraise why and how and where you lost customer, well you did not lose the sale you just received another lesson.

Lesson #C "Falling off a cliff". This is not much of a sales lesson as it is a life lesson when I tell them a story of a man out hiking and is walking along a narrow path and falls off a cliff that is 2000 feet high. The hiker gets lucky and grabs a branch and is hanging there.

"Help me, help me, please help me, is there anyone up there please help me" he screams but to no avail. He looks down to the drop below him and decides to turn to God.

"Help me, please God help me." And to his amazement a voice comes out of the sky in answer to his prayer.

"I am here, what is it you want from me?" The voice asks.

"Help me God, help me to live, don't let me fall, I will do anything you say" the hiker pleads.

"Will you do anything I ask?" The voice asks.

"Yes, I will do anything, just save me, I will do anything you ask" the voice comes back with a direct answer.

"Let go of the branch!" The voice demands.

The hiker looks down to fall he would take and without hesitation yells out. "Is there anyone one else up there?"

Point of the story is sometimes in life you just have to let go of your beliefs and just let go, otherwise take what you are learning in this class and mix it with your personality but believe that if you follow the steps, success is the end of the story. Just believe that following the system works.

Oh well, the nice thing about writing your own book you can stop anytime you want, and I have lost the feel for tonight, or is that it is 11pm, I slept all day and the poker bug just hit me and I want to go play, after last night's rush I been wondering if it is still there, so I am off to the poker room. I will end it with another up poem, I mean the original idea of the book was to show the reader of a poem what inspired the poet to write it, well I guess what I wrote today will explain my poem.

Valarie and I are beginning to see the success Real World Selling coming to life, we have created an Enterprise.

"THE ENTERPRISE"

It is real this time because I walked the walk

Success is at hand because I talk the talk

So don't think to big there is a way to go

Put ego on the shelf and show the show.

You have the goal now work the plan

You made a challenge now take a stand

And realize it come to this with a touchdown in sight

Time to put away the wrongs and do everything right

You have a super partner along with her being your best friend

Working together to find the happy road one that will not end

And even when the bumps come there is no way to
stop this team

A lifetime of togetherness and lessons are about to produce
the dreams.

CHAPTER 11

August 26, 2019 1:30 A.M.

Sunday was a tough day waiting to hear about my father-in-law Jimmy on how he is doing. The hospital has transferred him from Pahrump to Las Vegas and got him comfortable in hospice. Still hasn't been any luck on his kidneys kicking back in.

Sunday there is always a big tournament at the Muckleshoot Casino, today was $300 buy in. I got there late, and I played tight until I got pocket 10s and a guy raised three times the big blind, I just called. Flop 9-3-4 with two clubs, I like the flop and bet the size of the pot. The guy next to me goes all in, hum, I start thinking, he didn't raise before the flop. I just put him on a pair with a club draw, right now I am the better hand. I call saying what I thought, "You have A-9, or club draw." And we turn over our cards and I was right about both things, he has A-9 of clubs. An air ball on the turn, and he hits his club on the river. My $300 is gone.

Do I re-buy or just call it a day? No one is home and I did get sucked out on, but I also know when cards run bad to call it an early day. Nah, I will re-buy another $300.

Within 10 minutes I get pocket 10s again, no raise and I just smooth call. The flop is perfect A-10-6, no flush draw. I got a set of 10s. I should have checked knowing that if someone has an Ace they will bet, and I will check raise, but I make a small bet and two people just call. On the turn, 9 flops, good card, I don't put anyone on 7-8. I come out heavy, half of my chips, starting stack is $25,000 in chips, one guy folds another calls. I want the board to pair, but I think I am ok with my three of a kind, I get my wish, another ace, giving me 10s full of aces, I push the rest of my chips into the pot, the guy snap calls with his A-9, he makes a runner, runner aces full house. Now my $600 is gone.

Now I head home, thinking how poker sure its ups and downs has, Friday cards ran over me, I won eight hands in a row and $600 and today I blow it back. I am not mad on how I played the hands, but I am mad that I didn't listen to my inner self with my first thought of going home after the first bad beat. Yesterday I could do no wrong, today I would run sour no matter what it was going to be a losing day, I should have cut my losses.

I tell these poker stories as poker is almost one third my life. I seriously do not think there is a man alive that has played more poker than me. And this is my life story. Oh yeah life story, let's get back to it.

October 4, 1998

Well, when I left off the other day Real World Selling is on the top of the world. There was no stopping me now, Right? You forget who is telling the story, Mr. so close to fame and fortune so many times and he drops the ball guy. Yeah, that is me.

I could write two chapters on the four months that I worked Real World Selling, but the ending is like many of my dreams, I hit some bumps. I get discouraged, I lose the vision, whatever the reason, I do not complete the dream.

I think about another adventure I had when we lived in Utah in 1988, just ten years prior to this story. The business was called "One Call for All" I was a middleman for any kind of business that existed, well almost. The idea was I find clients for businesses by promoting that we are experienced at knowing which business is the best in their field. I found plumbers, electricians, chiropractors, babysitters, many types of business who were willing to pay me 10% of any business I sent them. But the dream died when it was too costly to get the word out to consumers. If only there had been an internet back then as there was for a multimillion-dollar business today, who does the same thing I was trying to do, yep, that business is called "Angies List."

Oh well, I guess I can use the poem I am about for both my ventures that failed.

"ANOTHER STORY"

So when is your spirit of yesterday?
Gone somewhere else to play!
Leaving behind yesterday's views
In search of some brand-new clues
But yesterday was looking good
This time you knew you could
And just like that it is a fizzled dream
Just wasn't as easy as it seemed.
So now I go back on the line
Selling cars I will do just fine
Where money pressures get eased away
Heading back to what has always paid
But failure is not my point of view
You took an idea and you carried through
Like many of your stories from the past
You made it work but it didn't last.

CHAPTER 12

August 28, 2019 2:30 A.M.

So once again I will say that this is my book, my story, and I can write anyway I want. I don't have to be qualified to express my opinion; all I have to do is express it. And tonight, I wish to dedicate this to special people. And to the subject of Life and Death, again with no credentials only my gut feelings to push me along.

So how do I celebrate the life of Jimmy Higgins, who went to join his love of life, his partner of fifty years, Sandy Higgins. How many stories have we heard when a long relationship happens and one of the partners dies before the other that it is really like they both died that day and the one who lives does so only to mourn until the day comes that they can be together again. They cannot feel whole without the other.

Today a man passed on that was very special. We have all known men like Jimmy Higgins that stands in a category of their own when it comes to pride. They never ask for a handout in their life, never wanted anything they did not earn. Sure, they had hard times and were maybe even offered help, but that pride was too heavy to accept a free meal.

Today a man passed away that was loved by so many and again this love is not there just because he lived and was a Husband, a Father, a Grand-pa, and a Friend of so many. Like his life he also earned all the love that flowed his way.

Today a man passed away that will be missed by many, but those that love him also know that it is also a celebration of his life and anyone who had the luck to know Jimmy, will know how much he loved Sandy and missed her form the moment she moved on. And please believe the celebration is being done with singing and dancing and the happiness of Jimmy and Sandy once again being together. What a celebration.

CHAPTER 13

August 29, 2019 1A.M.

Just got home from the Muckleshoot where I finished my sixtieth hour of playing in the live games this month which makes me $360 bonus, they pay you to play and for every twenty hours you receive $100, or they pay you $5 an hour. At the casino I am known as the Motengator, years ago, it was the Motengator Kid, but I was a kid then, that's how long I have had that handle.

Albany, Oregon, 1975

In 1975 I had the only legal card room in the state of Oregon called, "Albany Card Club Poker with the Joker", it read on the billboard. I found a glitch in the law; Card rooms were legal, but the catch was no city would issue a business license.

I was getting my hair cut and my barber said that he wished he was not tied up in his barber shop all day that if he wasn't he would open a card room. I asked him under the table card room? He said "No, card rooms are legal in Oregon, but no city would issue a business license to conduct business as a card room".

"So that is what I am saying, you mean open a card room under the table!" I responded.

"No, I would open legal one in the town of Albany, you see Albany has no business license code, so if it is legal in the State, you can do it by just opening a room up". I left my barber with my head spinning, how cool would it be to own your own card room, it would be like Disneyland to me.

I play poker at the Elks Club every week and one of the players was a lawyer, so I gave him $300 for him to check out all the legalities about opening a card room right here in Albany.

He came back to me in three days telling me that he saw no law that would be able to stop me as of right now, but the city could easily put in a code that says no card rooms. So, keep your idea on the cuff and say nothing to nobody and just open your card room. Now if the city puts in a code and you are already open, they would have to let you stay under the grandfathered law, so you would not only have a card room but an exclusive one. Oh, one other thing after you open your card room as a private club, actually charge membership dues. Because if they decide to mess with you that would mean they would have to mess with the Elks Club, and half of the city council are Elks, so they just won't mess with you.

"Thanks buddy, best $300 I ever spend." Now what I thought, I don't have any money, but I knew the perfect person.

I got with my friend Cliff Atchley who owned two adult bookstores, one in Albany and another in Corvallis, he was rolling in money. We also had a poker game once a week in his Albany shop. I told him what I wanted to do, and he got excited. He asked me how much I needed, and I threw out twenty thousand, he jumped at it and I had the money to me the next morning along with him as my new partner.

I found a fantastic location in less than four weeks the twenty thousand was spent and Albany Card Club opened up. It was a class operation. I had built a snack bar, put in two pool tables, a ping-pong table and six poker tables. Everything I loved doing was now in my new fantasyland. I hired two cuties, well one and my third wife Becky to wait on the customers we didn't have yet, but I was sure like the "Field of Dreams" build it and they will come. And I was right just from the sign that cost $4000 and spun around and read "Albany Card Club Poker with the Joker".

NOW OPEN!

It cost $10 to join and that was the membership. I charged $1.50 every half hour a girl would come around after a hand was over and say "Time" and the players would just put out a buck fifty, most would put out two bucks giving the girl a 50- cent tip. One thing about poker players, poker chips are easier to spend than money, you have a stack in front of you, two chips seemed like nothing, they were glad to pay and get onto the next hand.

Within 3 weeks I had an average of three games going all the time, open 24 hours, there were no rules. Ten seats at $1.50 times two-times an hour, times 3 tables that was $90 bucks an hour multiplied that by say 20 hours, games broke up around 4 am, yes, I was generating $1800 a day. The snack bar was producing another $500. I had six employees and I was living the dream, and word was spreading I could see all six tables being filled up within a few months. It would be double what I was making now. This was 1975 that is a lot of money.

This was the days before Texas Hold'em and we played all the Stud games, and Five card draw. I played every day but I gave more money than I took just to keep my players happy, except this on time.

It was a Pot-limit 7 card stud game, and I am going to cut this story short. At the end, the pot that had $4100 in it. Bill Bryer said, "Sorry kid, I got four 8s", two face up and he had two in the hole as he started to reach for the pot. Whoa Billy "I got 4 kings", one face up and I had 3 kings down. All Bill said was "That's a Motengator" and that is how I got my handle Motengator Kid.

It was two years later when I was in Biloxi Mississippi playing in a tournament when I heard someone say Motengator; I never knew what a Motengator meant. I looked at the guy who said it, but he wasn't talking to me. There was a break for lunch with a free buffet for the players when I saw the guy who said Motengator. I walked over to him and asked. "Hey, I heard you say Motengator, can you tell me what the word means?"

He looked me right in the face and in a strong Mississippi accent he said' "Motengator, oh yeah, that is and ol' bijou term for the biggest, baddest meanest alligator in the swamp."

CHAPTER 14

August 31, 2019 7 P.M.

So, what happened to Real World Selling? What happened to Albany Card Club?

What happened to your third wife Becky, not to mention your 4th wife Jodee?

You keep flip flopping; I can't stay up with you.

Well, I wish I had an answer or some rhyme or reason on how I am writing this book. I am hoping it all comes together before the book ends and every question is answered. But I am writer by the moment, what I am feeling right then, which journal am I reading out of now. What is in my head will come out better than if I go searching.

Then I wonder who the hell asked those questions at the top of the page, you didn't as the reader, or maybe that is why I asked, because I see the reader wanting to know. It could be I want to know, and I am using you the reader as a cop out. I wonder how many of my readers I am going to lose right as this point as they may wonder if I am talking out my ass.

All my ventures seemed like a winner to me I would always start off the total optimist. I have found out there are different classes of people me being the one who comes up with Ideas, and people who implement the ideas to reality. The secret would be to have both attributes, I wasn't that lucky.

April 24, 1999

Real World Selling has me all wired up, I am having classes, and placing salesman. I have 6 different weeks of outside sales events; I am getting calls from Auto Dealers I never heard of, yep. I have a winner after all.

A month before this I had given up on Real World Selling, after getting discouraged, but when Dealerships began to call looking for my services, Well I don't take much to kick start me again, I was back in the game.

"BACK IN THE GAME"

The start of new feelings, the start of a new pace

It is like life just keeps kicking in to start a new race

And it has been here before, but this time is some kind of change

The answers have always been there and that's why it is strange

So grab hold of the illusions of gander and fame

At last you are coming to terms on how to play the game

Just flow in the knowledge the paths that have been traveled down

The answers that come at roads end are the ones that were found

So applying all the past years to the future of today

The rewards of life's lessons are the ones that will pay

This is April, this is Dallas's month, he would have turned eleven years old.

It is my memorial month when I think of all my loved ones who past before me and all the questions of life and death and the reasoning of why.

There is only one answer that a person can live with, and that is acceptance and believing that is the way it was meant to be. But the thoughts bring about a poem.

"DUES OF LIFE"

To those who I loved and went their separate way

Paying the dues of life when they left that day

There are the grandmas and grandpas a father a brother
and a wife

And it comes about faster as time passes, the dues of life

And one day my bus will stop to give me my final ride

And I got no qualms because I lived happily before I died

The thoughts of Dallas are memories that are hard to fade

For wasn't he just too young for the dues he had paid

The day that the bus stops and takes me for my final ride
in the sky

I will come face to face with answers when we all come
eye to eye.

   What's Behind the Words?

CHAPTER 15

September 1, 2019 9 P.M.

Wow, summer just flew by. It is September already. But I got a feeling we are going to have an Indian summer like we have the last 5 or 6 years when the weather stays nice until October.

Well, we had the Tournament of Champions a once-a-month event at the Muckleshoot today, $20,000 in chips, I got 5000 extra for being one of the top point leaders, but it did no good.

There were only about 60 players and at first, I run good and build my stack to 35,000, but to make a long story short, I flop 3 threes. And Vu, one of the dealers taking the day off to play, made a straight on the turn and the board never paired so as simple as it ending in one hand, I was out. Didn't matter how good I played to get as far as I did, poker sometimes is like life, there are no second chances. Again, I learned not to slow play a good hand. If I come out swinging, betting a lot on the flop, Vu would have never called to make his gutter straight. But greed always sets in and I want to take a bigger pot, by sucking the players in, well it turned out that I was the sucker, some people are helpless when it comes to the way they play poker, and I think my game is not getting better in fact I think I am losing my advantage.

Don't think I will write much tonight because I am one tired old man, that's how I feel. I didn't sleep worth a dam last night and tomorrow we, me Val and a couple of our kids are going to go "Do the Puyallup" for you people reading this not from Washington I am talking about the Puyallup Fair, the biggest fair in the North West, I have been going for sixty years. I am just a creature of habit.

But since this is a book of poems also, I will end tonight's writings with the last page in my journal dated 1-19-1998 to the date of this poem ending the journal 11-22-1999.

"GOODBYE BOOK"

You were a friend I spent many hours with, I friend that will be there in the future.

I have nothing I have shared with you this last two years that I am ashamed of.

I feel only advancement in maturity also closer to my family and in life.

Accomplishments were real and pleasing and in more ways than past journals,

And you were most rewarding in the earnings of the culprit known as money.

Now at your end I just wanted to say thank you friend for being a good listener.

And thanks for being there with your new, fresh clear page for me to exchange my inner self.

Goodbye book

CHAPTER 16

September 3, 2019 4 P.M.

The Bahamas are getting washed away, the Hurricane Dorion is heading to Florida to do much damage in its Category 4, 140-mile winds format, and I think about Rose Foster Lemco's 68th birthday tomorrow. Why I wonder. What hold does she have over me; after all she has been dead twice as long as she lived, dying in 1972. Our son Shane is 51 years old, and she was my first love, my first wife. We fought and argued all the time; we had very little in common, but we sure clicked when it came to loving.

She was one bad ass woman, one time in 1968, we were at Slims Drive-In hamburger joint by Daffodil Bowl in Puyallup when I put my Coke up on the dash of my new 1955 Chevy Belair and it fell getting all over my loved car. I jumped out cussing and some dude says, 'Ahh, that's too bad."

"What did you say, punk!" I come right back at him super pissed.

"You heard me asshole!" he snapped back.

I was twenty years old, didn't mind a fight and this was just the cause I needed to take out the anger of me spilling my Coke. I was doing a pretty good job kicking this guy's ass, I am sure he felt confident when he first saw my 5ft 5in body, but don't ever underestimate a small guy. But then two of this guy's friends grabbed me and this punk was hitting me when all of a sudden there was Rosy with a 12-inch crescent wrench. She comes down hard on one of guys head, his knees give out and he collapses. She catches another in his hand, stopping a hard blow that was heading for his head.

But the look on his face says the blow was still painful. The guy I originally was fighting decides to high tail it and runs away. Rosy and I decide to get out of there before the cops show up.

And that was Rosy my first love and who I think about right now forty-seven years after her death and wish her a happy birthday.

Now I will go pray for the Bahamas and Florida.

CHAPTER 17

September 4, 2019, 3 A.M.

What's behind the words has me in a zone that I am not sure about. I just think it is not really a book but just some guy rambling on, and then I think so what, it sure not about money, and I am kind of enjoying doing it.

So, let's make it about my grandkids wanting to read about their grandpa and that is enough reason to be writing my life story. I have a few fans who like reading the stuff I write, if you have been reading along with what I have been writing then please say so; it really helps me to want to continue.

Nah, that's B.S. I am doing this for myself and heck with what the world thinks.

I just came home from the Muckleshoot where I had a losing day, $120 in the tournament and $300 in a 1-3 spread game. I ran unlucky, but that is an excuse bad player use when they don't win. Truth is I am a fantastic player that has been running unlucky. It all comes in the form of proof at the end of the year when you tally up your losses for the year, and take them away from what you won for the year, and like the last fifteen years I have always been on the up side.

Poker I feel is an 80% luck factor game, 20% skill, that is quite advantage having 20% in your favor. Casinos don't make 20% on any of their games, but the volume they do ads up to 9% average on all money that is bet. And I would love to have that action just one day a year.

Well, I am about to go to my closet where all my journals are, but not in order. I reach in not looking and what journal comes out will be the next pages of my book. I could look and maybe try to make sense to my story, but I have come to believe you as the reader are just along for the ride, as I am, and like my life let fate take control. But not until tomorrow as I am off to the Thursday night tournament, wish me luck. Oh, it is now Sep 5th, 5pm time just spaced me by.

CHAPTER 18

September 6, 2019 2 A.M.

Well, I just got home from the Muckleshoot another losing day. I did pick up $360 for the hours I played in August, sixty of them in total and came home with $100 more then I left with, which means I lost $260. Oh well, not starting off September too good.

I went to my closet and grabbed a journal, and I came out with my longest journal I have 300 pages covering the date September 21, 2006 until July 6, 2011. So let us begin.

September 26, 2006

Wows, big book, don't know if I will fill an entire page, probably will write two times on one page. I won't be alive to finish this book, so this is my last book; this will make thirteen journals I have totaled.

I just got my last disability check of $960; they say my funds are exhausted. It was a great run and I have no complaints knew it had to end sooner or later. Now I go for Social Security disability and I will get a lawyer to go for the settlement. Anyway, knowing I got my last check and 10K still in the bank. I am here at Pechanga Indian casino paying $59 a night on a room. Been here three days and I am down $1000, but $400 is what I lost in slot machines, how stupid is that?

I have enough money to live through November and then I don't know what's going to happen, but how sweet it has been for the last sixteen months, retired, doing what I love the most, poker, then some more poker, TV and movies, then some more poker. I have done alright overall being ahead over $40K, along with over $40K in workman's comp, but you sure need a lot to live in San Diego. I have spent over $50K on rent.

Lord, here we are in a new book. Thank you for getting through the last book. Devin is healthy and coming home safe from Iraq in two more months. Drew is living back up in Seattle, Destiny and Dane are doing well in school and love living in San Diego.

And me Lord, I just want to thank you for my health. I know I do not do anything to deserve good health, but you keep letting me go on. Why I still ask myself, do you have a purpose for me, you just name it I will do it. Oh well, I better get some sleep, I got poker in the morning.

"THE DREAM IS OVER"

Well the dream is over and gone clean out of sight

And I became sober seeing I have lost what is right

So I don't give a dam seems I am out to destroy

I am back to the scam just where is the joy

The worlds got cold and that is too bad

Seems I lost my soul and that's pretty sad

So I am all done just get out of my way

The nice guy is gone; the new is out for the pay.

I wrote that right before I went to prison almost thirty years ago, July 21, 1977 to be exact, don't know why I wrote it now, other than scamming on workman's comp, which I don't feel guilty about. But it comes to an end, so be it.

I feel guiltier about how I am living my life, I have far more potential than I use. Is it that I am just a get by type of guy, that I have all I need, and no one ever has all they want that I just choose getting by; being content where is there a higher high then being content?

CHAPTER 19

September 6, 2019 6 P.M.

I just got out of bed; I ate some broccoli cheese soup poured over mashed potatoes and a glass of apple/grape juice. There is no tournament at the Muckleshoot on Fridays so it looks like I will spend my night writing.

I wrote last night until 3.30 am, and then climbed in bed knowing I won't fall asleep until 6am, my norm. I get on my Facebook and some of my friends are blogging saying how they have insomnia, and we talk back in forth. I have come to the conclusion that because I fall asleep at 6am and don't get up until 4pm, that I don't have insomnia, it is normal not to fall asleep until fourteen hours after you wake up. Oh well, busy day ahead, let's get started.

October 1, 2006

Poker has sure done me well the last year and a half. But now I do not have any income because disability is no more. My cash is down to $5K which is good for one month living in San Diego.

Quinsey Power Sports, the reason I moved to San Diego and gave up Lemco Motors in Buckley three years ago, to run their motorcycle dealership said they would hire me back. But not at the same salary I was getting before my accident there, but from $12,000 a month to $8000. Still a great wage but my ego won't let it happen.

I am thinking about selling time share after all you know going in that time share is a con-game, and me well I am a conman, sounds right down my alley.

Funny how poker or really just one hand can make a difference in life's outcome. Or bottom line what needs to be done because if the one hand would have been different, chances are I would have taken the tournament off and won the $10,000 or at least got in the top five which started at $8000 and worked its way up.

Hate bad beat stories but this is worthy of the telling. We are down to four tables of ten we begin with in a $300 buy-in tourney. I have 120K in chips. I get a KK in the big blind. A guy with the same amount of chips as me goes all in before me. I don't have to call thinking he could have AA, but no, he won't go all in, he wants callers if he has aces, he will bait the pot but not all in, I call. A guy behind me with a short stack pushes all his chips in, no doubt he wasn't thinking very clear as he called with a Q-10. As we all turn over our cards, the guy that went all in shows his K-J of spades, I proudly show my KK. The flop is Q-10-6, turn a 7, and river a 9, they both beat me as the man yells "yes" when he made his straight on the river.

Oh well not the worst bad beat story I ever heard. But now I don't have much of a bankroll and I got a family to take care of. Drew came in last night and needs some help, he got married a few days ago and has already broke up, I will go talk to him when I am done here.

I really thought my body would give out before I had to go back to work and Val would get the quarter million life insurance, I have on me. I sure don't treat my body as a temple; in fact, I don't treat my body with any kind of respect. By all rights I should have been dead by now. It is almost like I have a death wish rather than go back to work.

I still have the settlement for my injury at Quincy's with workman's comp; as usual I keep looking for the easy way to gather cash.

I will go get the story from Drew on his marriage then come back and finish writing for today.

Like father, like son. Drew is having a good time in Vegas when he meets this girl. She is a rich girl, well her Mother is rich, and they get hammered and she says let's get married, in Vegas you can get married in an instant as in Reno, where I got married my first three times. Drew says OK. They go and buy some rings, head to a chapel and they both say I do. They wake up in the morning I guess they never consummated the marriage, so he says it is not official. Drew leaves and has a free gold ring as a trophy. I guess Drew never saw that girl again.

Reality creeps in and I am off to job land. I am hoping I get the timeshare job in hopes they don't do much of a background check, as you can't get a timeshare license if you are a felon. I will just lie.

"TIME SLIPPED AWAY"

It is kind of funny how time just slipped away

Like 58 years seems like one long day

Yet a lifetime has come and it is almost gone

Thought I'd be a king but I ended up a pawn

I was going to climb the mountain but I lacked the drive

Seem all I really wanted was enough to just survive

The talent was there I would say that for a fact

Knew I was a good writer, I knew I could act

So I waited for the knock at my door, which was my game

I waited and I waited but the knock just never came

Now regrets seem to have slipped into my life

My only real accomplishment was my 5th wife

And 6 children has to be some kind of feat

But as a father I would have say I was pretty weak

And if being lazy and doing things your own way

Won you a trophy, well then I got paid

So I guess I am giving up, I will blame it on fate

Just kick back and wait for the pearly gate
And hopeful that God will even let me in
Done so much wrong, but I confess my sin
Yes Time just came by and it just slipped away
But I had fun a lot of fun that much I will say.

CHAPTER 20

September 11, 2019, 1 A.M.

I could do a long blog about 9/11, but I am sure there will be many postings on it, and from people who have stronger feelings then I do, so I will leave to them to bring out "we Will never forget" in you. I need a little excitement, so I am going back to prison in my journal rather than 2006 which I was talking about my last posting of my book; we are heading back to 1979 and Salem State Prison.

November 16, 1979

"FRIDAY NIGHT"

*The flush echoes the night mixed with sounds of
morbid laughter*

Bragging from the wannabes who forgot what they were after

Eyes follow a sneaky badge forever on the watch

Can't be caught gambling or playing with your crotch

The click of the dominoes the shuffle of the cards

Convicts telling yesterday's jokes someone is playing a guitar

A smoky room with cable view will hide unneeded hours

But views of foxy ladies do not help lost powers

So exit for this is party night first one this week

No sense getting greedy you already had your peak.

What a fight tonight over something dealing with pride but that is what most fights are about here anyway. Tonight, it was

Brad 6 ft 3 inches tall 215 pounds against Willy 5 ft 9 inch 170 pounds. Willy is watching a TV show in the rec room when, want-to-be bully Brad decides to change the channel without asking anybody. Brad knows he was out of line, but no one will confront or so he thinks. Willy is a cool guy another bank robber like me, so we get along fine. He is a thinker, had a much better plan then I did, and he got away with it, which is always a good plan. But the bank teller remembered a tattoo on his neck and that is how he got busted.

It was because of that reason I never got one tattoo because like fingerprints all tattoos are recorded and many crimes are solved just by a tattoo on record. Really, I never believed in tattoos anyway. Let's go back to the fight.

Like I said Willy is a thinker and he knows he is not going to lay down to what Brad just did, in Willy's mind it was like Brad was calling him a punk. But Willy knows he cannot go face to face with Brad who even though he is bully, he is pretty tough one and much bigger.

Willy makes like he is going to leave the room; Brad checks him out and thinking this guy is just going to let it go. Brad looks around the room; one guy says, "Hey we were watching that.

"So," Brad says back giving the guy an evil eye. "Just telling you, that's all," the guy answers back which tells Brad, no fight with this guy. Brad sits down with the remote in his hand totally confident that he showed everyone who the boss is.

A glass coffee mug smashes into Brad's head sending him flying out of his chair to his knees, he shakes it off just in time to see the foot that smashed into his nose, he shakes that off also with blood pouring from his nose. He jumps forward grabbing his culprit around the waist. Bad move, his nose is too close to Willy's knee, Brad grabs Willy by his hair and pulls it right into his upsurge knee right into his already bloody nose which is now broken by the force of the knee to it, and it also knocks Brad out who falls on his back out cold.

Brad is lucky that Willy is a cool guy, like I said; rather than going further he just turns and walks away. Not far the cameras got the fight and guards were there to meet Willy

      What's Behind the Words?

and he was marched off to the hole. Brad was taken to the infirmary unconscious, as he never woke up until he had a cast on his face.

Willy will spend a week in the hole, and it will be dropped with no charges against him, Cops also despise bullies and when they get the whole story, which they will, they will just write it off as prison justice.

"NOTHING TO LOSE"

The conqueror stood before a crowd of fear,

His delightful smile brought no cheers

"My servants" he spoke as he raised his hands

I come forth to tell you my demands

Bring your riches and lay them at my feet

All your cattle and grain for me to eat

Your virgin maidens are mine at will

And you leaders come forth so I may kill

The conquered peasant bowed his head

Thought what he being asked is worst then death

With one impose the dagger flew

Splitting the Conquers head in two

The moral of this story if you so choose

Don't threaten a man with nothing to lose.

CHAPTER 21

September 11, 2019, 8 P.M.

Here I sit at home rather than in the 7pm tournament because I have been running so sour. Last night in the tournament my AA got beat by A-Q, then I went to a live game and bought in $250 and played for two hours, while I waited for a hand I mean, just wasn't getting any cards and in two hours I blinded and called to see a flop five times never getting a hand, which brought my $250 down to $150.

Ok I finally pick up QQ on the button, it is $10 to me with four people in the pot, I make it $90 being happy if they all fold, and I will pick up $50. One guy calls me. The flop comes 7- 8-4 with 2 hearts, the guy sees I only have about $60 left and he goes all in, I got to call and he says, "Good call I only have a draw" I turn over my QQ, he turns over his A-Q of hearts, the turn comes a 10, he has only an Ace or a heart to hit, sure enough a 7 of hearts on the river, I head home thinking how in the tournament and the live game, I got busted both times against an A-Q.

So, I have time to spend with Valarie, did some honey do's, and now I will write a little, not a bad punishment. Let's head back to prison.

March 22, 1980

Jodee is having a hard time and share of troubles, she has been sick for ten days, she got in a car wreck, only the car hurt luckily and today she got laid off from her job and she is hurting for money. We been married one year now, but there is nothing I can do for her my gambling is way down.

So, who do you suppose came to her rescue, nor other than the white night, my little Bro, Steve? He loaned her $500. Why is he so good hearted and me so corrupt?

Steve spends time with Betty Brown, head of the parole board, who tells Steve she would be talking to Judge Woolridge about my sentence. Remember I got forty years to begin with and Steve with all his personal input has already got the consecutive sentence changed to concurrent so now I am down to five years. Mostly Steve's doing along with the lawyer he hired who got my sentenced moved from consecutive to concurrent.

Two years ago, when I needed to know how long I would be in prison there was no one who could answer so at the same time I have turned to religion and Jesus Christ, not sure if I was for real or just looking for a cop-out.

I asked before I opened the bible "Lord, tell me how long I will be spending in prison." And I open the bible up randomly, and as God is my witness my finger was on the words, 1260 days and the story was about a battle and how long it lasted. But if ever a person needed a sign, it was then and that there was no other answer then God who led me to 1260 days. I believed the answer.

Every twelve days would equal 1% of my time and every twelve days I would post a new date of how much time I had left. As of this day I had at the top of my page 971 down vs. 289 days left= 77% over. And I believed it, I had less than a year left to go. And if the prediction comes true, I would never doubt Jesus Christ again, as he had given me all the proof I would need.

I still have my love battle going on in my head how can I love so many and for any of them be true. Can you love more than one woman? I knew I loved Dee Dee, I write her telling her of my love for her. Yet yesterday I wrote to Becky telling her I still loved her. All this while I am now married to Jodee, who I am about to write a poem to in hopes that it does something to cheer her up and something for our one-year anniversary.

"THE CREATION"

The God of contentment raised his hand
And cracked he had but one demand
The couple we choose will have the gift
To forever provides each other's lift

God of time was quick to see
That they needed a couple who will forever be
A oneness deep inside the two
That no mortal man could undo

God of the heart master of feeling
Knew their loneliness needed healing
Bringing together a call of fate
A love of love no longer waits.

The God of Happiness said with pride
We shall bring together man and bride
They will cherish life's true treasure
A total Happiness beyond any measure

And God of love master of all
Spoke his words in final call
We need to do nothing, except make them meet
For within each other they find life's treat.
Once in a lifetime comes true love
Created by the God's high above
And one day they will discuss
The perfect Oneness, is the creation us.

What's Behind the Words?

CHAPTER 22

September 13, 2019, 2:45 P.M.

It is Friday the 13th, do you believe in the old wise tale that it is unlucky.

You couldn't prove it by me as I just came from the Muckleshoot Casino. Where I got 7th place in the tournament then won $250 in the live game. I guess I could blame my KK getting beat by Q-10 that put me out of the tournament on Friday the 13th. Poker players are funny creatures when it comes to superstitions, it could be the lucky coins they bring, or they have a lucky seat or table, many believe that different dealers bring different luck, me I believe that knowing when to quit is the best luck to have. If you play as much as I, do you will know when you are running good, or bad, doesn't matter if you are running good, you know that eventually the cards turn, time to take your winnings and walk away.

Or if you're running badly, you just know it, when you wait and wait for a hand and you are card dead. You watch the flop to see if you are throwing away any winners, but you're not.

My dad who was a great player and one of the tightest I have ever seen had a rule. Do not play a hand until you have thrown away a winner. Sorry dad, I get a good hand I am playing it, and then when my nut flush doesn't hit, or I flop three of a kind and get beat by straight I the say dad you were right, I should have waited until I threw away a winner. But bottom line when you are running bad, chances are it is not going to change.

The nice thing about living five minutes from the casino, is there is a game tomorrow, it isn't going anywhere, come back tomorrow. So more important than lucky charms, is control your wins and losses.

I feel sorry for people who are reading my so-called book who do not have the slightest Idea what I am talking about and have never played poker.

I also feel sorry for anyone expecting me to write some more on my story who are not going to get anything today as it is 3am, I am tired, so I will finish with poem, not one from my journal or one I ever know, it will be what I write right now that comes out of my head as fast as I type.

"OFF THE TOP OF MY HEAD"

Don't expect a miracle or even anything good

If I get lucky and words come, well knock-on wood

Maybe I won't rhyme or even make any sense

And I am the last to worry about sounding dense

See I really don't care how it will all come out

Maybe better than the hot dog I ate with sauerkraut

I have to be crazy to eat this shit at night

But I was hungry and 7/11 was open so it seemed right

I put on the mustard and some Jalapeños too

Now the heart burn begins like I haven't a clue

So pop in a Tums and I will try to sleep

Today is just one more memory I will keep.

So good night all my friends, and go to sleep smart

I end my night with this hotdog and Jalapeño fart.

What a funny creature Facebook is and how many friends I have hooked up with because of its creation. You hear bad things about Facebook because of the power it has in reaching so many people.

Today I hooked up with Mike Morris who now lives in Lacey, we met in Tacoma at the Sizzler Steakhouse at the end of 512 freeway. Valarie went with me. When both Mike and I were sixteen we would go down to Sumner Bowling alley, yes Sumner had a bowling alley until the word is the owner, Ron Dittimore burned it down for insurance in the mid-60s, he later took over Daffodil Bowl in Puyallup, anyway, sorry getting carried away which is Facebook's fault because they have a way of bringing back memories. How many times you get a notice about something you posted years ago, a photo, a get together with the people you love, and it restores memories you have just forgotten about. To me it is like a charge to my memory buds. Oh yeah, back to Mike Morris and the Sumner Bowling alley. They had pool tables there also and one or two times a week Mike and I would go play pool, or we bowl a few games, Ron Dittimore liked me and would let me bowl all I wanted for 25 cents a game, he thought I had potential as a future bowler as I carried a 182 average at sixteen years old, this was back in the day that bowling was pretty popular. Oh yeah, we were talking about Mike Morris and meeting him at Sizzler. We did today at 1 pm, I told him I had a doctor's appointment today about my blood tests I took 3 weeks ago. How come it takes three weeks for the doctor to tell you your results? But I told Mike we could meet later in the day about 5pm after my doctor's appointment, but he asked if we could meet before knowing and living in Lacey how bad the traffic is between there and Tacoma, so the 1 pm meeting was set up.

Now I had not seen Mike for over 35 years, we had been friends on Facebook for about four years and we kept threatening that we should get together, but it never came about, Then I seen how Mike liked my writing and how he had encouraged me to keep it up. And two days ago, I sent him my phone number and said let's just do it and so here we are at the Sizzler.

We were both born in 1948 him in May and me in August and I tell him how I respect my elders he has a cane. He is not as tall as I remember but he is slumped over from the cancer he carries. He tells me how five years ago the doctors said if he did not get an operation, he would not make it very much longer, but if he gets the operation, he will be bed ridden, He

---

says no, I will take what I can get, now five years later still able to drive walk with the help of a cane, but LIVE, yeah, Mike you made the right choice. I can tell he is in pain, but he tries not to let on, Valarie, Mike and I have a great lunch and trade jokes and stories, we all wished he would have brought his wife of forty years but neither of us thought about it. I didn't think about Valarie coming until this morning. We make plans for the four of us to get together sometime.

The whole point of this whole story is about memories, and life and to say thanks to Facebook as you just supplied some memories, a hug from an old friend, and this stupid post, yet I feel like I do about many of my posts that others will be helped in some sort of way, it's my story and I will live with my version.

What's Behind the Words?

CHAPTER 23

September 15, 2019 7:30 P.M.

Well, I am home too early to have done any good in the Sunday tournament, My AA got cracked again. I think from now on when I get AA, I am just going to push all my chips in and quit slow playing it, if no one calls I will take a small pot but that is better than losing all my chips to a suck-out.

I am glad I am home as I have a post I have been thinking about all day. It deals with the enemy of most of us, the ugliest word to all us humans, the word is CANCER.

There are very few people cancer does not affect if not you personally then someone you know and love, like my brother Steve just recently. The story very seldom ends happy. That is where today's writing is going; yes, for once I want to celebrate a happy ending.

I am going to tell you about my friend Stacy Ganson. She is one remarkable creature.

I am not even sure what kind of cancer Stacy had, not that any are good, but hers was bad enough for her to battle with it for a bunch of years, getting chemo, being sick, having her whole life turned up-side down, but battle she did. I mean she got in the ring with Mohammad Ali and George Forman at the same time and kicked both their asses, that's how much of a battle it was.

Imagine many would have given up or just lay down and died before putting up with all she did. But Battle she did, no way was she going to lie down, she saw a light and kept reaching for it.

I followed her on Facebook for the past years when she is in the hospital tubes going every which way. I watched as she slowly went bald from the chemo treatments and still the photos all had a smile on her face.

You want to talk about positive attitude, well look it up in the dictionary and there is a photo of Stacy, she kept a good attitude. Determination, then mix that with the luck of having so many people that loved Stacy and who prayed for her. Then go back once more to her determination.

Then there is Don Ganson, Stacy's husband who did the whole ride right alongside of her, the true hero of a man that lives by his vows, "For better or worst."

And Stacy's son Colter who has showed how brave he is when he is around his mom but cried when he was alone, knowing how much he loved his mom.

How many times I talked to Don and me asking how Stacy is doing and he tried to hide the words that it doesn't look good the best he could.

Alright are you ready for some fireworks, some Hip Hip Hoorays. That's my girl, a story of one in a thousand; ok here is your answer.

Don and Stacy are going on a cruise and when they get back, they are going to Venice all-in celebration of Stacy no longer has cancer.

God, I love happy endings.

CHAPTER 24

September 16, 2019 5 P.M.

So, it is a nasty rainy day if I wish it to be, but no, I am an up- side type of person and I will find the good in this glorious day, Hum I think I just did. I am alive, I feel good, I love life, my family, my friends, and I have enough money to get in tonight's poker tournament. So, stick your rainy nasty day where the sun don't shine, I am out to make the most of it.

That was something I wrote on my Facebook page and thought why not share with the book I am writing about myself. I spend a lot of time on Facebook; I have about two- hundred followers. I have a hard time staying away from politics and the dialog sometimes gets ugly. I am feuding with a friend I have had for over fifty years and I have blocked Shane my son because of stupid politics.

All I will say in this book is that I am not a Donald Trump fan, and as Forrest Gump says that's all I am going to say about that, other than it is not worth the grief,

Now it is 1 A.M. on 9/17/2019 and I just got home from the tournament getting knocked out four before the money after five hours of play. Ok. A little more about prison life then I think I will crash for the night.

January 24th, 1980

I have no collage today because there is a heavy fog, won't be any yard that's for sure. I guess they think it is a great time to make an escape, oh well can't be too careful.

Sunny McCain came back today with a 60-year sentence with a minimum of thirty years for robbery and rape. We were in county together and he would say how he screwed up and just wanted another chance with his wife and baby, and he received his chance and only did two years of a ten- year sentence for theft. He had been out less than six months and now he is back, for it might as well be a life sentence.

Now I can't even associate with Sunny because of the rape charge, rape puts inmates in their own category "Rapo".

I heard that he was robbing a house when the door downstairs opened; he hurried and hid in a closet. It turns out it was the seventeen-year-old daughter coming home from school. Sunny watched her from the closet as she undressed to get out of her school clothes. The excited stupid bastard came out of the closet and raped the poor kid. Well, he got what he deserved.

When you are locked up all day long it gets to many people, your more tense, you lack patience, and you are mad at the situation and it is easy to strike out for the slightest reason.

It started between some black and white guys over, I am sure something stupid, but a push turned into a shove and then fists flew. Then others joined in, the whites unlike most prisons outnumber the blacks three to one in Oregon so in case of a race riot the blacks would not stand a chance. About ten inmates were fighting as the guards rushed in yelling everyone to lie down, if you don't do as they say you risk being hit with a night stick or pepper sprayed. The ten fighters are marched off to the hole. Chow is ended and everyone is sent back to their cells. It is just one of those days that you accept when you are in prison.

That's fine, you make do with each day the best you can, Bobby and I play pinochle and dominoes most of the day as usual Bobby loses and ends up doing push-ups for his loss. I think how I should be the one doing pushups as Bobby is already twice as strong as I am.

We get bored with each other and decide to read, I am reading a book about an explorer when I get an urge to write a poem.

"TRAVELER"

The vessel the mind the Flying Dutchman

Touches the Pilgrim propelled by the wind

An explorer, a pathfinder, a dangerous nomad

Reaches out for that thing no one else has had

To discover that which has yet to be found

A Columbus to prove not flat, no, the world is round

Ulysses, Gulliver, or a wondering Jew

A mountain a desert or ocean blue

A homeless wonderer or immigrant straggler

A searching soul or Gypsy rambler

Combined with the lust of the search

To have the treasure of being first

Reaching a goal before they die

Just one answer to the question why

Isn't it grand that they existed

Or many of our truths would still be mystic.

CHAPTER 25

September 18, 2019 1:00 A.M.

Gees I just have a hard time winning with pocket Aces the other night I swore I would not slow play them again, so when I got them tonight three people had called when the fourth raised the pot by 3 times and I just said all-in. The other three folded and the guy that raises snap calls with 88, and what comes on the flop, a damn 8. Last night I got beat by two running cards the only out they had, and it hit for them.

I am starting to wonder what I have done wrong to deserve such treatment, but it narrows down to the old saying "That's Poker" hard to live with sometimes but what other choice do I have. I went home and record the loss into my journal then decided to come to my computer and write a little.

I cannot believe the complaints I have heard about the rain, which has been pretty bad the last two days, but let's not forget we live in Washington and we just got over fifteen weeks of a wonderful summer. Take a look around and see all the green which stays that way for ever, hence the Evergreen State. I just talked to a friend in the Midwest who had 90 degrees with 98% humidity. Yeah, give me Washington weather anytime. Oh well let's head back to prison for our night cap tonight.

January 29, 1980, Salem State Prison

Drugs, I have done more drugs in prison then I ever did on the outside world. It is the old story of high mark-up three to five times above street value. They come inside in many different ways. Some are pretty disgusting, when they get a visit, the inmate is slipped the drugs wrapped in a balloon from their visitor, he then swallows the balloon and then once back in the cell if it is soon enough, they shove their fist down their throat and throw them up with the hopes the balloon comes flying out mixed with all the puke. They are then washed off and it is ready for business.

The second option is even grosser, the inmate cannot barf them out and must wait for the balloon to past through the system then retrieve from his bowel movement. More than once while I served my time an inmate died when a balloon of heroin busted in their stomach.

Many drugs are brought in by corrupt guards who can triple their money, I had such a source, and my drugs were sold as shit proof and they lined up for my drugs knowing they weren't in someone's shit.

My guy was a thirty-year veteran working in the prison system who had realized with his retirement a year away that he was short of having enough to retire on. I am sure I had something to do with him changing the way he felt as he totally trusted me that if something came down I would not give him up. He was right as I would do forty more years before I would become a snitch. Along with my silver tongue about how easy it would be for him to make the extra he needed for his retirement.

He told me once that he had seen other guards who were working the system driving new cars, lived in bigger homes, but he had held out knowing it was the right thing to do. But real-world slips in and like most of us; we do what we have to do to survive. As for me I was doing pretty well for an inmate, I had gambling, football pools and for a short time I was in the drug business. Jodee, my fourth wife, is receiving money every day of the week from wife's, friends and parents of inmates, the inmate is given a phone number they give to their outside source to call and the arrangements are made for payment.

Prison officials know most of what is going on, but I think the fact that drugs make for a mellower prison, especially weed, that they overlook it. I never figured out how it went on so much inside prison there was no way the officials were fighting it.

So now you know why I did more drugs in prison, lucky for me I was afraid of doing heroin for I could have had all I wanted but seeing what the evil drug does and that 25% of the people that were inside these walls were here because of that drug, I specialized in weed and cocaine. Not for long even with the free hand I had, there were still risks and when I remembered the value of freedom along with a friend of mine who was snitched off and was busted and got ten more years, well I gave up the drug end of my business.

I traded some weed for acid I mean some good acid LSD 25, in a sugar cube the original Timothy Leary stuff, I tell you I saw people climbing up my pee stream when I was pissing. I heard sounds coming from out of toilet, yeah, I had a buzz on, I just stayed in my cell hoping no guards were going to ask me anything as I was wishing only to get back to normal. I pulled out my journal and this is what I wrote, if you figure out what I was trying to say, let me know would ya.

Walk with me, talk to me, sudden feelings live in life's fate

Grass grows where the sun is shone and yesterday's questions are tomorrows whys

I listen for a message to shout its way, walk with me talk to me

Ice is forming outside one walkway slipping and sliding.

Whispering voices are fading away, what, do I do for snow to wash away?

I fear not the sight for I long in truth and I am protected. Yet fight I would

A shadow casting wrinkling rain, the stage is set only for the performers

And memories drop the curtain, opening up to today's orange sunshine

For I am, for what I have done and been and seen

I am the Lion of a Kingdom within the palace of the mind.

　　　　　　　　　　　　　　　What's Behind the Words?

The smile of laughter harder to find

The pit of the heart is as yet is harder to stop

For I will be what is yet to happen for I once was what I remembered

And I wouldn't change either for the other, or another, good night mother.

CHAPTER 26

September 18, 2019 6 P.M.

Not often I write during the day, but I am not going to play the Wednesday tournament as it is a satellite for the upcoming Fall classic tournament and I won't be in town, I am going to be on a road trip with my beautiful wife and driving our G.M.C. Arcadia.

We have never gone on a road trip before our plans are for seven days to just travel take our time. We will stop and see some relatives in Oregon and head to a wedding in California. Then put the cruise control pointed at Las Vegas, you did not think I would leave Vegas out, did you? I won a free seat in a 150K free roll poker tournament at Planet Hollywood on the 14th of October.

nce again, I wonder if this entry is something I want in my book, would it interest readers that I am going to go on a road trip and again I will answer, too bad it is my book, I have come to the conclusion that it will not be a blockbuster and that maybe our grandbabies might want to know that after thirty-seven years of marriage that their grandparents are going on their first road trip.

Funny when I think about what I just said and in the next verse I am going to take my sweet innocent babies into prison. Oh well my story kids, tag along if you wish.

July 21, 1980, Oregon State Prison

Everything I am about to write is word for word out of my journal

3 YEARS

Man, it is 100 degrees, well I waited for summer and it's here Hello, hot huh!

Last year at this time it did not seem like I had been down two years already, now a year later and I feel the same way. Yet I still remember when I push open the screen door of the Banker's home with a gun in my hand, it seems like yesterday. I don't think I was as scared as I was excited, a kind of excitement I never knew.

I remember my first feeling when I saw the bag full of money the Banker brought me. How nice things were going to become, the load off my shoulders because of this money. Of course, the way I lived I would be broke again within three months. We would have had a lot of fun though.

I remember my first feelings when I first spotted the F.B.I. I remember trying to outrun them; I remember the feeling when I thought we had lost them. Then the final feeling when we were caught in the middle of the street and shotguns with what it seemed like cannon ball size barrels pointed at our chests. Yeah, I remember it all. And now I know the feeling of being in prison for three years.

Many changes in my life since that day exactly three years ago, Yay, it's my anniversary. I think there are more good changes then bad, Na I don't think so, I know I am better off just in my attitude, the only bad part is when it comes to Shane and my family putting out hard earned cash on lawyers. I have money being held by Jodee that will be repaid when I get out but if I paid them while I was in prison, they would be worried about what I was up to make money in prison.

1096 days inside the walls seems longer when you say it that way.

I played Reggie Smallwood handball today after he told me he was done gambling with me, but he lost two cartons to me first. I won another three cartons off another sucker in handball who never figure that handball is an easy game to hustle; if you are the better player, you can always make the game close. Get them to play another.

Well, I am glad three years is over, wish it was four years, but like the other three it will go fast and by then I will be on parole.

And I think of my day it is more like summer camp then prison, I worked out on the weight pile this morning after a good breakfast, played about ten games of handball.

Tonight, I have a softball game that has over one-hundred cartons bet on it, I had to give up two runs. I am pitching which I love doing I have made up my batting order and I am not too afraid of losing tonight.

After the game I will head up to the Rec room and watch a movie, use the telephone to call Jodee, if the movie is no good, I will go and play pool.

Yep, that is doing hard time in prison, like I said before if there were women here, I might never leave.

Happy Anniversary!

What's Behind the Words?

CHAPTER 27

September 19, 2019 10 P.M.

Well, I am home too early to have done any good in the tournament. Could tell you another bad beat story but what difference does that make, I forget to tell you the story how I broke my buddy Glen with a 4/6. Yep, poker players only want to tell you a story when the cards went against them and forget how they sucked out also. The bottom line is the end result and tonight I lost.

It is my Mom's birthday tomorrow I will go to lunch with my sister and any other family member that wants to come to celebrate her 94th birthday.

Have you ever thought how life is about destiny that things that happen have a reason in order to bring about a future? It is like someone cutting in front of you and they are hit by a car that would have hit you. That even something as big as World War 2 would have a meaning, a reason, that something good could come about because the war existed.

I guess thinking about my mom makes me think about how my mom and dad met because of the war. My dad from the Bronx N.Y. to meet my mother from Sydney Australia would have never happened if there had not been the war. Sorry just a crazy thought before I head back to prison.

August 14, 1980 Oregon State Prison

GOOD BY O.S.P, Good riddance.

These will be the last words I write behind the wall; I am being sent to the Forest Camp tomorrow.

Three years and three weeks since I have known freedom, but that is really just a frame of mind what freedom is, even though there were bars and walls, I still felt as free as I could. I got my AA degree, I learned, hopefully some writing skills from all the English and writing classes I took. I picked up a 4th wife who loves me and could be my lifelong soul mate. And the biggest lesson I have learned is the value of freedom. Yeah, it was like I just attended college, and it cost me nothing for room and board and all the schooling. Almost seems wrong for all the law abiding people.

All the guys did there check out with a hard punch in the chest. That is how they say, see you later, nice knowing you, see you in the fall if at all. Good-bye.

I will miss many friends I had in here, way more than I had in the free world, and more loyal, many of them would have killed for me that is kind of ugly to say or think but one thing I have learned, the truth is the truth.

I will really miss Bobby; I plan to see what I can do for him to get his twenty-five-year sentence reduced once I get out.

Well one thing for sure it has been a trip all along.

"ALL ALONG"

Well oh jolly friend in your mystic trip of life

You must feel it was time for me to move along

Thanks for the ticket for where it is I go

It is time for me to wonder a different road then one I have known before

For you are the driver I just ride along

To places I am sure you mapped out long ago

And I ask not the why's to where it is that I am off too

Never needed any pushing for where I have been, I just tag along

My thumb was out when you stopped to give me the ride

And never once did the wind stay long in my face

For rainbows kept their pace all along
All along, it has been a trip all along.

CHAPTER 28

September 20, 2019, 7 P.M.

We had a nice lunch with my sister and Valarie celebrating my Mom's 94th birthday. We cracked up over a story we told about Mom who all but lost her hearing so I got her a pair of hearing aids, wanting to see if it helped my Mom's hearing my sister Terri asked Mom, "Mom can you hear me?" Mom looked at her like she didn't hear her, "Mom, Mom. What color are my eyes?" my Mom quickly replied 'Blue, what color you want them to be?" I guess the hearing aids worked. But it cracked us up.

August 15, 1980 Tillamook Forest Prison Camp

NO WALLS NO MORE.

Yep, I now live in the town that makes great cheese, well way up in the woods not in the town. Son of a bitch I made it away from the walls and my first day is going just fine. No pigs messing with you, a TV, pool tables. Foosball, a swimming hole, a ping-pong table and all the sally I could smoke (Sally code word for weed), no bars, and no 4pm counts.

Maggot is here and gets me in his 4-man cabin; most are eight men that is a real plus to have ½ the amount of people to deal with. I hear about how sweet the visits are and how my chances to consummate mine and Jodee's marriage is not hard to do. This is the most exciting news I have heard in three years.

I mean sex is on most man's mind at the age of thirty-one, but I don't think I am bragging when I say out of all the things people enjoy doing, like I love to go bowling, play pool, even as much as I love playing poker the one thing, I love more than any other activity is good old fashion sex. For three years I have been without, to hear there is a good chance to having sex with my wife of a year and a half, how often we would write each other fantasies in our letters about when we finally get together how it would be out of this world. I cannot get it out of my head, and it is only three days before Jodee can visit me.

I call Jodee and tell her the news; I get excited that she is as excited as I am it is going to be a long three days.

I get the bad news about how hard the work is here at the forest camp, and this is the middle of fire fight season, 15-hour days, sleeping on the ground and being a regular mountain man. I being a city boy and lazy at heart, my idea of roughing it is getting a motel that does not have cable. I will find a way out of it; I know I will.

As of right now I am loving it a nice bed the food is twice as good then what I have eaten the last three years and the people all seem more mellow. It is a little colder here being up in the mountains but I hope to be gone by Christmas. No one tells you when to turn your lights off. You do have to get up every morning at 5:30, I will get used to it.

Wild deer wonder into the camp and flourish from the food the inmates feed them, we have three cats, the freshest air I have breathed in my life. There no longer the rattle of keys that was constant inside the walls.

Jodee gets to come the sixty miles to visit me up to six times a month from her place in Portland. Wow it all hits me at once that this is just what I needed in my life right now.

I called Shane and when he hears we can toss a football, play a game of ping pong go for a walk in the woods, he gets all excited as I am to do these things with the person I love most in the world. Shane is living with my brother Ed, his wife Velma and their three girls, Linda, Laurie, and Lisa. He has everything he needs except a mother and father, but he is a tough kid and is dealing with it well for being eleven-years old.

It is my 32nd birthday tomorrow and when I get here there are three birthday cards from Jodee, they play poker here, so I know right away where my commissary is coming from and won't be a problem. Yeah, the change is great and may take a few days to sink in, but tonight I sleep in a regular bed with a big fluffy pillow, great shower room, and silly little things that you don't give a second thought about, but it becomes pure luxury when you have been without.

I just feel everything changed today, all to the good the beginning of uphill all the way, I am home for a while, I feel a beautiful peace flowing through me. Thank you, Lord.

"BORN LUCKY"

Sure like everyone I started as a child, I was different with a streak of wild

I looked to the wind to guide my path I bow to the sun that made me laugh

I was off to the meant to be…..

I traveled roads with many turns stayed to the right avoiding burns

Stopping here and there just to look and see what is left for me to be

And I was glad that I was guided……

I asked no whys to the why it is all so, seeing no reason I needed to know

I laughed and smiled the whole way through never once knowing what I was to do

And coasting on the waves of life has been my total existence………..

I thank, I shout, I make a plea so glad that I am me

For the answer was in plain sight for me to see. You see my friends I was born lucky.

                                     What's Behind the Words?

CHAPTER 29

September 21, 2019 11:30 P.M.

I wrote the below part earlier today and posted it on Facebook. The replies I got is the reason I am writing right now, they encouraged me to forget about the editing and just write and worry about the editing when the book is done. I feel I should share what I posted on Facebook as it was in me to do it and this is a book about me, my feelings and thoughts should be shared. So, I did it, my choice.

I have been editing "What's behind the words" I don't like it; it is so time consuming and I hate to see how many errors I make. It has kept me busy all day and hasn't done much else; maybe I should give it up. I have my son Drew who is a teacher and English major, he has already done some editing, then My niece Linda also a teacher says she would do the editing. And I appreciated them both and if I thought the book had some commercial value, I would reward them when royalties start coming in but I don't see a blockbuster or even close so it would not be fair to them for all the hard work involved. The other answer is to say piss on the editing and publish it as it is since I am only doing it for a select few that in years to come will even care that I bothered to write it at all.

Guess I am in one of my down moods today, editing does that to me, I will be fine tomorrow.

August 16, 1980, Tillamook Forest Prison Camp

A thousand times better birthday then the last three I have had. It was a beautiful day from 6am this morning to right now, everything was fantastic.

Jodee was here all day in fact she was here an hour early thinking visiting started at 8:30 rather than 9:30; she was here all day until 3:30. We had lunch together and I had French fries for the first time in three years. We sat on the lawn all day, we talked about the plan two days from now when I would meet her in the woods for a day, I am sure will never be forgotten. We talked about so many things; not once did we have to search for something to say the conversation just kept coming.

After Jodee left I walked up into the woods scouting out a spot to meet up with Jodee, in two days. Oh, I forgot to tell you that it has to be on a day that a certain guard works that you can be gone from the camp to have a get together with your lady. $50 seems to make this guard blind and this is the only day that he works days, and a person can pull off a lover's visit.

Nighttime comes the deer come to our lawn, for the second night I look up to a full sky of stars, it is all sinking in, I am here and I love it.

After dinner I play poker and I win $20, and then win three cartons of smokes playing pool, I let the guy go for one carton and now he knows he owes me a favor. I have a bunch of friends here some I knew in the joint and some new ones.

I worry about myself in the sense that I don't get too lax and keep pushing it to the limit too often. If I do get busted, please let it be after Jodee and I get together.

Well Happy Birthday kid, 32 years old, wow you can't call yourself kid much longer.

My third day without the wall it is still sinking in when I wake up, I am not sure where I am.

Little fantastic brother Steve came and seen me today. What a brother, for three years it was like he did the time with me, how much he helped with reducing my sentence I will never know. I do know he put his heart into everything he did with only one thought in his mind and that was to help me. I will never forget what I owe him.

I guess the real test of this place starts tomorrow when I begin work; I was given a pair of work boots to wear. I have never had a pair of work boots in my life; in fact, I do not think I have ever done physical work in my life. I have to go pick out a hard hat later and hear tell they give you a pair of suspenders also. Wow, it is starting to scare me what the hell is going to happen tomorrow.

Guess I got out of O.S.P. just in time they have a hunger strike going on, everyone locked up over a snitch being stabbed to death. Oh well bring on tomorrow. I'm ready.

"TOMORROW, TOMORROW"

And it comes with what is meant to be and I shiver with its comings

And what are scared about your acting like a kid about to enter a new class

What will be, is going to happen and your worried now about the future

Just look back a few days ago in your past tomorrow is way brighter

Ok, ok I ill shake it off with a vision that tomorrow could be something good.

You see how easy that was because you changed your attitude, yeah smart move.

Come on tomorrow you don't scare me, bring it on I will kick your ass. Better son, much better

CHAPTER 30

September 27, 2019, 7 P.M.

Ego! How much of the driving force is brought on because of ego? How does the fact you feel good about something that it will make you do better at what you are trying to do? Yet too much ego can get in the way also, if that makes any sense.

Is ego like a diet and you need to portion it? When I was teaching sales procedures, I would go over ego with the management; I would tell the managers that you are really nothing but ego herders. I would tell them that a salesman's criteria are 90% ego and 10% bullshit, if you deflate the ego of a salesman all you have left is the bullshit. Pump up the ego to get the best performance. You got a bone to pick with the salesperson save it for the end of the day, let them be pissed on their own time.

Sometimes when I am playing poker ego becomes a downfall for me, if I pull off a fantastic bluff my ego wants to show everyone how good I am, and I show the bluff. When really all it does is give the other player's information about your play, and sometimes because of my ego I play my bluff to the max and come out with a large bet in hopes of the other player will fold but instead they call. Are they calling because they were at the table when I showed an ego bluff before? So yes, there is a downside to ego.

Another bad ego point is bragging how good you are, ego is like karate "He that knows does not tell, he that tells does not know." You are the only one that needs to know how good you are.

Now why all of a sudden why am I preaching to you about ego, well because of my ego I have not wrote for a week. The last time I wrote only two people tuned in on that post, I am sure more read it but forgot to push the like button, but it bothered me that my writing had lost interest that people can care less about what I have to write.

Now it is a week later and the only one who suffered was my writing because of my ego. I had forgotten that I write for myself and for my grandkids that will one day want to know about the life their grandpa lived. So goodbye ego for now I am heading back to prison and if you the reader wants to know what I was up to before this post you will have to scroll down and find my past postings. I am no longer out to impress you; I have gained control of my ego.

August 19, 1980 at Tillamook Forest Prison Camp

Boy I made it through a day of work. I was the gas man, and my job was to keep the crew in gas which meant going from one hill to another and when I say hill, I should say mountain and carrying a 5 gallon can. Wow are they out of there mind I never worked so hard in my life. I was tricked into the job when the boss man told us of the jobs that need to be done and he also offered the job of the gasman and he made it sound easy, so I raised my hand and got the job. I guess all first day workers fall for the job. I won't be raising my hand tomorrow.

One thing that I think happened today which could help me to get a camp job was that the boot on my right foot that had an operation when I was kid and left a scar started bleeding from the rubbing of the boot. I will see if I can play it off.

It is all planned for tomorrow night after work for Jodee to meet me in the woods and we will consummate our marriage, it will be a hard day at work having that on my mind all day.

It is a week today that I have been at the forest camp seems so much longer like inside the walls was a lifetime ago. I haven't done anything constructive since I been here, I have not written a letter or a poem. I haven't picked up my guitar one time. But the good part is I am doing the most important thing to do while you are in prison. I am doing time and boy it is just flying by.

"YESTERDAY'S TOMORROW"

When it has all been thought of sometime before

You wished and hoped that there is so much more

When mistakes scar and leave their mark

And the lightness known turns into dark

When tears have dried and washed away

And the talking is done but you have more to say

When all the laughing runs into pain

And sunny days bring on the rain

When all is balanced the happiness with the sorrow

Then today will turn into yesterday's tomorrow.

CHAPTER 31

September 28, 2019, 5:30 P.M.

Greta Thunberg the 16-year-old climate change girl is building momentum in the news the last few weeks. I truly believe that climate change is a natural occurrence that has been going on since time began but I also believe that man is escalating the process. So, enter a young little girl with gumption and the fortitude to tell why man is helping to move climate change even faster.

We are hearing the stories of the garbage in the ocean and lakes causing an un-balance and affecting the aquatic creatures. How different types of algae are showing up caused by pollution, we have heard how the reduction of rain forest and the reoccurring forest fires that are now more common than any time in our history. The natural disasters are more consistent than ever, the rising sea level causing flooding as ice caps melt.

It is Greta Thunberg that brought about these thoughts which I could live without; I enjoy life too much to have to think about such things. But isn't that a cop-out for my grandchildren that it may not be my problem, but it sounds like it will become theirs. But then I wonder what can I do about it, and what has all this got to do with me writing about my life and I have totally flip-flopped on my train of thought.

I was watching the news before I sat down to write tonight, there was a story about this young girl and how she has caused a movement all over the world that are encouraging young people everywhere, millions of young kids to wanting answers and bringing awareness of the issues that are going to become young people's problems in the future.

Now I remember what I wanted to say. A paragraph back I wondered what I can do about the problems and the answer is I will do nothing about it. But God Bless activists like Greta for it is people like her that bring change. And her courage to speak before the important older folks of a room full of decision makers who she feels could be doing more than they are, she yells at them "How Dare You."

I guess since I am writing about my life the flash thoughts that run through my head are part of who I am.

August 20, 1980, Tillamook Forest Prison Camp

Today is a day I will remember the rest of my life. Jodee and I consummated our marriage. After a year and a half of marriage we united tonight in holy wedlock. Laying on a blanket in the woods it was so beautiful, so real, so needed.

Yet now lying on my bunk with three other guys in my room snoring and farting while I write of my first love making in three years has a way of losing the romance. Then my thoughts go back to just an hour ago and I think of Jodee and her nakedness. Boy did we eat each other up all our anticipation and everything we talked about in our fantasy letters to each other all come into play in our two-hour session. It all came to sweet life tonight; it was like a reward we had both earned. I would like to go on, but tiredness is starting to kick my ass, I have to get up in six hours and today was harder than yesterday. I carried forty pounds of seedlings on my back going up the mountain planting them with a shovel in one hand. My foot was bleeding worst then yesterday, I showed the watch commander who seems to like me, and he said he would see what he could do.

I begin to drift off and my thoughts go back to the love making and when I ask Jodee do you want to get together tomorrow. She instantly said yes. And I think, there I go again pushing it, going to the limit, and knowing me, I will continue to push to I use up all the odds against me and get busted and sent back to the walls. My oh well attitude kicks in and my accepting what's to will be but I will get in all the licks and enjoyment I can until the inevitable happens.

The next night:

What have I done so right to deserve all that is given me? I am so lucky, it is not luck that I am able to do the things I do, there has to be more to it than just luck. Everything that comes my way is because I am looked over and I hope it is God and not the devil that is doing the looking.

Yes, Jodee and I got together again tonight; it was more erotic than last night. Came really close to getting busted also, if the patrol car would have turned right rather then left, they would have had me.

Jodee also brings me an ounce of weed that cost her $180 that I will turn into $700.

I get back to camp just as the watch commander opens up the door to my cabin and gives me the news that starting tomorrow, I am on the camp crew, my job will be mowing the lawn, weeding, and keeping the bathrooms clean.

Yes, life is good.

"BRIGHT AHEAD"

*Hey misty wind, how you been miles have pasted
since we rapped*

*Doing just fine thought I would drop you a line to say I no
longer feel trapped*

*I have lost all sorrow I can see a bright tomorrow as bright as
the beasts fire eyes*

*The water is not deep, the mountain no longer steep and
yesterday left all the lies*

*Green lights ahead and fluffy soft beds wrinkles are from the
smiles on my face*

*Well thanks for your ear I am sure I will see you there I will
give you a little taste.*

CHAPTER 32

September 29, 2019, 5 P.M.

Here I sit at home after watching the Seahawks kick the Cardinals ass 27-10. I am not a big football fan, but I do follow the Seahawks, I think it is Russell Wilson I like to watch as he is a great quarter-back but to me he is a true man's man a special type of hero. If you are a fan, then you know what I am talking about.

Here is an example my nephew Kingston is five years old with cancer he is fighting for his life he needs a bone marrow transplant; he is sitting in Seattle's Children's Hospital when who shows up to give some encouragement but Russell Wilson. Russell doesn't just stop by with some well wishes but he spends time with Kingston and talk about many things. Russell stays in the hospital most of the day spending time with many children. This is not a rare thing; you can set your clock by it; I am not sure if it is Tuesdays or Wednesday, but he is there every week and spends the day with kids with cancer. The year the Seahawks won the Superbowl the kids were told that Russell may not make it in for his normal visit. Well, that is not how Hero's work, he is a full time Hero and he showed up that week also.

Hero's what classifies someone as a hero; they come in all shapes and sizes, from all walks of life. They give of their self, they put others before themselves and they don't even know that they are heroes. Russell has all the money he needs I am sure he could find better things to do, but that is my thinking, not Russell as I feel he gets more satisfaction from what he does at the hospital than anything else he could be doing. And that my friend is why he is a Hero.

Another Hero we have up here in Seattle is Bill Gates who gives away his fortune to so many worthy causes. It would take pages of writing to cover all the Bill and Melinda do for people all over the world, but if you want to be impressed and see why he qualifies as a Hero just goggle him you will be impressed, but mostly in my eyes he is a Hero because he sees wrong, he feels other people's agony and he has the resource to do something about, and he does. Bill Gates is a Hero.

We have all heard stories of the soldiers that jump on grenades to save the life of their brothers, or a guy like O'Hare a pilot who took on 9 Japanese fighters by himself to save a ship from being boomed. These kinds of Hero's are in a league of their own they had no plans to become a hero, but the true hero just responds without thought when he feels the calling.

Then there is the all-America type hero that will even go through suffering to help another. I dedicate this piece to the following true to life hero. His name is Nick Estrada at the time he is eighteen years old, and he hears about my nephew Kingston not having much time left if he does not receive his bone marrow transfer, he has never met Kingston, knows nothing about him yet he wants to help. He is not sure if he will match what Kingston needs and there must be an eight out of ten matches to try the transplant.

Nick goes and takes a test and what do you know he is ten for ten match, the perfect match. The procedure is set up as soon as possible, it is quite painful and hours in the making, but this kid, this 18-year-old kid saved the life of my nephew. And Kingston today is active in all sorts of sports. You have to call his parents Zac and Rachel heroes also as they stuck in there never giving up hope and now three kids later, they get to watch Kingston play football.

God bless all the heroes; they are beyond special.

Now I feel funny going from the story I just wrote to going back to my prison story where I left off last chapter yesterday, but it is the price of being a writer.

August 29, 1980 Tillamook Forest Prison Camp

Wow, I became activities director for the camp. I am given $300 to give away on the Labor Day events as prize money. So, I decide to come up with events that I am good at.

Chess, Pool, and ping-pong, but as it turns out I cannot participate as I am too busy keeping track of everything. I really enjoy doing it and I now have become the most popular guy at the camp which may not have happened if I had played in the events as I would have won them all, not bragging, just the participation is really weak. I didn't need the money as I sold the entire ounce of weed Jodee brought and had $700 stashed. I have moved into a two-man cabin with Terry we get along great, he has been at the camp longer than anyone and knows all the ins and outs.

I enjoy my job even cleaning the toilets, sinks and showers; in fact, I do an excellent job. I am looking forward to having a get together with Jodee during the day, I have the freedom and there is only I guard on duty when the whole camp is out in the field.

I knew Warden Cupp was coming for an inspection, so I do a super job on all my jobs. He is being given a tour and is in the laundry room which is behind the toilets. The ceiling has a gap between the toilet and laundry. I climb up on the sink and speak through the gap in the wall.

"Warden Cupp, this is God, I want you to give Lemco a pass!" The Warden who I am sure remembers when he was on board when I gave my famous "I was passing my bowels" speech, again gets the pleasure of my humor, not that it did any good as I did not receive my pass.

I spend a lot of time with Officer Steve Birdsing he is really a cool guy for a cop, no, he is a cool guy either way. We spend much of our time exchanging poetry we have wrote. I know in the back of my mind I am feeling him out on how if I leave the camp to meet up with Jodee how he would take it. I never stop looking for angles I can't help it; I think it is in my D.N.A. My real goal is to get to use his trailer he lives in parked at the camp now that would be a score.

I am looking forward for tomorrow when Jodee brings Shane.

I am really sore from playing touch football yesterday, because it is not touch football after all the times players would say, you didn't touch me, until Ok, I will tackle your ass and there is no augment. I do my share of tackling with my small frame but the old saying, "The bigger you are the harder you fall, does not offset the smaller you are the further you fly."

Well, another long yet enjoyable day here at what I consider my summer camp.

Shane's 11th birthday is just a month away I want to write him a poem.

"SHANE'S BIRTHDAY POEM"

My son on your 11th birthday, I have some words I wish to say.

You're at that age where you begin to understand starting your journal of becoming a man.

I have no gifts that I can give only these word by which to live

Never be mean it is better being kind it will give you a better frame of mind

Never steal or tell yourself a lie wait until the fight is over before you cry

Never cheat your family or your friend it would only make feel bad in the end

Remember when you quit learning or you will quit growing it is not the end as long as you seek knowing

So learn as much in school as you possibly can, it will come in handy when you're a Man

Remember to enjoy life with smiles and laughs choose the happiest roads as your path.

Most important thank God every day for all the good he sends your way

And always know this my loving son; your Dad will love you until life is done

---

CHAPTER 33

October 1, 2019, midnight

Poker is such a big part of my life and I truly feel I have played more poker than any man in the world. Probably not true as it is a big world but, in my head, I believe it. I think about me playing since I was a kid and then graduated once I turned 21 and could play in casinos. I am 71 years old, and I swear I have twenty years of my life at a poker table, what a waste of time, what a stupid life I have lived. I think of if I had used my poker energy to anything else. Real estate for instance, with me having the sales ability I have I would have been fantastic and no doubt successful. I always wanted to be an actor, what if I had used my energy in making something happen in the acting world.

How stupid this conversation is I am 71 and it sound like I am having regrets, and me who always preaches you are what you are through experience and let's say I never played poker, well then, I would have never robbed a bank, all the lessons I learned in prison and would of never came about, and prison made me appreciate the value of freedom. You really don't know what you have until you lose it.

A few chapters back I was talking about my Mom and World War 2 and if that war would not have happened, I'd have never been born. Well, it is the same thing here with me wishing I had chosen a different path. I cannot change the past so today becomes an acceptance of who and what I am, and I am really ok with who I am. In fact, if you weigh life by contentment which is the best of places a person can be well, I am the richest man in the world and have received the top prize. The trophy

Contentment is the world's biggest prize. Well let's head back to the prison camp.

October 27, 1980, Tillamook Forest Prison Camp

Jodee and I just had our 13th time together this afternoon. I prefer us getting together in the day rather than at night. It is starting to get really cold up here in the mountain. I have been here ten weeks now and the camp is pretty much mine. I have so many keys I am starting to feel like a cop. I get to use the kitchen all night long if I wish, I got the key. Not many nights when I don't have a peanut butter and jelly sandwich washed down with a couple of glasses of milk. I can play pool all night or watch TV; I have the key to the Rec room. I have no schedule as long as my work is done, Sarge, the captain of the guard, doesn't give a shit when I do it, just make sure it is done. I take pride in how clean I keep the bathrooms and people have quit spitting in the sink after I kicked a guy's ass that kept doing it. I am no tough guy, well maybe I am, but if you piss me off, I am not one to wait for the other guy to take the first punch, it is going to be me throwing the first punch, then a second and a third usually with kick thrown in and the fight is over. This is only my third fight in three and half years and so far, I have come out on top on all of them. Besides, I am so well liked that if someone was to get the best of me a whole crew would jump in. I guess I am kind of a chicken shit also because I know I cannot lose a fight as help would jump in before it got bad and when I decide I need to fight I do it when the crew is around. It also is 2-fold when I kick some one's ass who is usually much bigger than me, well I earn a lot of respect. I have been a scrapper my whole life I think being small brought it out in me, I always wanted to prove big things come in little packages and I always took my size personal. Like if a guy flicks a buddy with his finger behind the ear, well mostly it is done with fun, not me, I would think I got flicked because I am small and I would strike back.

I always hated bullies who I feel are nothing but punks or they wouldn't be bullies. I was always fast to stand up to a bully knowing they like to pick on the defenseless and they hate to be hurt, Me well, I didn't mind pain it makes me fight harder. And 95% of fight I ever got in I always got the first punch in. Sorry got carried away talking like I am some kind of bad ass when really, I am a real mellow dude.

The camp had a change of guard today I guess word was out how lax things are out here. It is going to be harder to get away to be with Jodee. These new cops have no clue that I run the camp but when one of them comes over to me and demands my keys back and says, this place is changing as of today. I figured they knew something about me to even know I had keys. The cops name is Ackerman and is a true asshole; power-tripper and I can tell right off he is going to be trouble.

The new cops show up with two buses full of inmates, the word is they have been ordered by the courts to bring down the over-crowding inside the walls. I hardly know any of the new inmates. And when they turn the four-man cabins into eight-men and put mattresses in the Rec room to accommodate the camp now becoming overcrowded. None of what happened today is good, the changes are bad enough, but attitudes have gone from a mellow camp to stressful one.

Maggot who just had his cabin double its size in people comes up to me. "What the fuck is going on here Ronny, this is total bullshit!"

"Your right about that, brother, that asshole cop just took my keys, talking about how things are going to be changing around here."

** Editor's note, well my note, to the reader I am about to talk in realistic lingo, and you must remember we are prisoners and this is the 80s, but I feel I would be doing my writing injustice to not tell it how it was, along with the real feelings.

It is not the way I felt, even in the eighties, but it is the way it was, **

"Did you see how many niggers they brought up here today? We never had so many here in the year I have been here, you know what happens when they bunch up and start doing that nigger shit talk and act like they are special, well It won't happen here, I'm telling you this is not going to work out." Maggot kept rambling on.

"The cops tried to move a nigger into our cabin, can you believe that shit want us to sleep with a nigger, me and Eight Ball, kind of pushed him into a corner and told him that he don't want to be in this cabin, and he better go talk to the guards about bedding down somewhere else, he got the point and took his gear and left."

'Hold on a second Maggot, it ain't that bad I only counted eight blacks, one of them I know he was on my softball team, with the three blacks already out here, well that is eleven total blacks and with eighty whites and Mexicans, well they won't start no trouble." I saw where this situation could end up and I was going to try to slow it down before it got out of hand.

"I am going to go talk to Sarge and hopefully I can get him to see what could happen and for him to stop anything before it starts. Talk to you in a bit". I headed to the command post to talk to Sarge who was really a Captain and in charge of the camp, we got along fine.

"Hey couch how da fuck you doing?" It was Bishop the black guy who was on my team.

"Alright Bishop Ol' Buddy, I am surprised to see you out here, thought you had life?" We met in a friend like embrace with a quick hug and a shoulder-to-shoulder bump. I watched everyone's reaction I heard someone behind me say nigger lover. I turned and looked and saw it was Harvey and I knew I would have to deal with that and him but not now.

"Yeah, well you know life don't mean life especially when the prison is crowded, god dam I did life, fucking eighteen years, that is my life, so what's the scoop on this place Couch, is it cool here, I mean eighteen years I been looking at a wall I never thought I see so many fucking trees again, I mean its fucking beautiful here." Bishop talked as I looked at him and the last thing on his mind was any kind of race shit, he wasn't looking for any trouble, he was just happy to be here, which reminded me how I felt just a little over two months ago. I saw Sarge on the top of the porch watching everything that was going on.

"I got to go talk to the man Bishop, I will get with you later, I will show you around and give you the whole scoop" I started to walk away.

He put his hand on my shoulder and said, "I feel the tension here Couch, we not looking for no trouble. We just want to be free, as free as I have felt in eighteen years, we ain't looking for no trouble, understand?"

"Loud and clear brother, just stay easy I am going to see what kind of fixing I can do. Not that it is broke yet, but before it needs fixing." Bishop's eyes looked right at mine and I saw the trust he had in me, made me feel kind of proud, we each gave a nod to each other.

"Sarge, can we talk?" I asked as I walked up to him. "Sure, Lemco, right here or you want to go into the office?"

"Let's do the office" I said, I was happy that Sarge was showing me this much respect.

"What's cooking Lemco?" Sarge said as he sat behind his desk and I sat in front.

"Do I really need to tell you Sarge, your one smart Captain and you saw and felt the tension ever since the busses showed up right?"

"Yeah, what can we do about it?" Sarge snapped right back.

"Well for one thing you can't inter mingle the blacks and the whites, some of these white boys are pure Aryan Brotherhood, we would have a killing before the morning, a few of the blacks are true ghetto, anyway it would work out if you move the new black inmates into their own cabin, there's eight of them so that's perfect, the three that are already here have fit in fine where they are at so no change needed there. I stopped talking to see what I was saying was being heard, and Sarge with no hesitation said.

"Yeah, we can do that," Then Sarge reached in his desk draw and pulled out a pack of smokes and offered me one, which I took, as we lit up, I cracked.

"This is kind of like a peace pipe, huh." He laughed.

"One of your new boys took my keys; I am ok with it but why." It was just like me to push just a little more. Sarge looked at me as a smile grew to an all-out laugh.

"Lemco you are the funniest person I ever met, ever since you got here, what's it been a couple of months, you run around this place like you are the Warden, in a couple of days after coming here you get the camp job, you are beating all these young punks out of there cigarettes in every game you play with them, everyone here kisses your ass. You sneak into the kitchen whenever you want. You think you are so smart because I let you get away with sneaking off to get together with your wife," My jaw dropped, I went into shock. Sarge went on.

"Yeah, I knew and I didn't care, you were a great camp worker, you run the camp because all these inmates respect you, I don't understand you look like a little dip shit, but you do it" He went on after a little snicker, "Anyway things changed, when Jeff Humphries got busted bringing a pound of weed from my camp into the walls, mix that with the overcrowding, and yes, things have changed. This new crew of guards that just got here won't let you get away with your shit, I won't come down on you but if they bust you, your busted I won't stand in their way. Ok let's go get the camp in order." Sarge stood up and I was still dumbfounded over him knowing I was getting together with Jodee, and he never said a word or did anything about it, well I had to tell him.

"Sarge" I said and stopped so he would look me in the eyes. "What" he asked.

"Thanks, you are one classy guy!"

"Yeah, sure, whatever" He answered as he made his way out the door knowing what I just said, I meant.

"IN DISTANT PAST"

When it all begun sometime in a distant past

When time was eternal, yet it crept by fast

The now was here just a short time ago

Yet the future never really seems to show

Waiting is a game played by a select few
While others looked on for the slightest clue
Tomorrows parted for coming days
Leaving yesterday in some forgotten haze
And boring if known is a state of mind
Exciting is in what is yet to find
Experience is that which you have done before
Knowledge is for those who seek some more
Easy comes to them who see no hard
Put all their trust in the fate of God
Cruise through living as if it were a stage
The script of life has no last page
Play any role that is wished to be
A hero riding into a sunset free
A vision thought of is a vision seen
Using the past as your playing team
To enjoy living is life's only task
And it all began in some distant past

CHAPTER 34

October 24, 2019

I haven't written in over three weeks; writing needs some kind of inspiration and I seemed to have lost it. How life is going makes a difference in how inspired a person can be. I can't say I was on a bummer, but poker has a way of causing mood swings and I am sure when the cards seem to turn against you, this has influence on a person's mood.

I am speculating for the reason of going three weeks without writing when really, I have been doing things like being on the road for ten days with Valarie. It was kind of weird us driving over 3000 miles after so many years of flying anywhere we wanted to go because of Valerie's job and free flights.

It was really nice us spending the time together as a couple, we had a wedding to go to in California. It was one of the neatest weddings I have ever attended as it took place in Calico Ghost Town and the couple was married in a saloon right next door to the jail. We actually camped out one night, well if you call having a cabin as camping out. No TV, so that is roughing it, right?

Then it was off to Las Vegas and a poker $150,000 tournament I had earned an entry in. It was kind of a joke as the Casino gives this promotion to bring players into their casino and it worked as there were over 3000 entries, so the structure of the tournament was kind of a joke. You received $1500 in chips with blinds going up every twelve minutes, so it was just a shootout, as it turned out for me, I played two hands KQ of spades, and AQ of Diamonds, won neither hand and was out never taking one chip.

So, I go and play an $80 tournament, and this is what happens.

It is funny how life works and how fate admitted or not plays a big part of everyone's life. I was in a tournament at Planet Hollywood when a break came up. Me, I can't sit still for the ten-minute break and go to the slot machine, when a guy at my table sits next to me and lights up a smoke.

Now I'm into my month-long fight of quitting smoking. I look at this man as the drag from his smoke eases into his lungs and I can almost feel the sensation as the spot that gets pleased by that rush of smoke hits the pleasing zone. "Can I bum a smoke?" I ask him.

He gives me a light after I rip off the filter, he doesn't ask me why but just lights my smoke. Ahh, the rush is still there as I take a deep puff.

We begin talking about poker and the rush I am on; I think I was chip leader at break time. We trade names with a handshake. His name is Jason Rockwell Gale, and he is the founder of Shark Media Group, LLC and he develops web pages. I tell him I need a web page for my novels and ask if he could put something together for me for $500. He says yes, he could do that. I was to find out after pulling up his web page that he charges up to $10,000 for his expertise but never told me that.

I have a good feeling about Jason, and I pay him the $500 right then that is before I pulled up any information about him, I just went with my gut.

Turns out his company (Quite big really, he has sixty designers) but they are Computer wizards, yet Jason seems to be doing everything firsthand on my project. He told me when I give him the money he would call me on Monday, that's today and he did as he said.

He has already got me my site ronlemco.com. The only thing I know for sure, I will not sell my books just waiting for people to find them. Now I will have a way to promote, and the dream is still alive thanks to fate and the meeting of Jason.

I posted that on Facebook last week and just copy pasted it here it is worthy to be in my book.

Funny how my so-called book is going. I for one, have no idea I just keep going and I haven't touched 10% of the poems

I have written. So, I guess I will just play as I go along. I will end today's writing with a poem I wrote three years ago which kind of explains the mood I am in.

January 27, 2016

"NO YIELD"

Somewhere are the memories of long forgotten poems

The places I used to go when my mind was free to roam

*The upbeat bouncing younger man with a brain that
knew no yield*

Back when I used to climb mountains now, I settle for a field

There is no room to complain downhill is not always bad

*Some would say I am showing grief but really, I am just a
little mad*

*You see Youth is wasted on the young; back then I
had no time*

*It was always the future I saw, and all the visions
looked just fine*

Now that I stop and think if life was one long line

*It seems I won all along the way and I am cashing in
on my prime.*

CHAPTER 35

October 29, 2016, 3 A.M.

Well, here I am just getting home from a night of poker. My life revolves around poker. I lost tonight to a bad beat in the 7pm tournament when I flopped three 7s and a guy with an open ender raises all-in to my small bet doing just what I hoped he would do. I call and we turn over our cards, the flop was 7/9/4 rainbow. He has 8/10 of spades, no spades on the board, he pushed all-in on a draw and I turn over my pocket 7s. The turn is another 4, and the river is a 6 which makes his straight. Some would say he played bad, but not really. When I made a small bet, it invited him to make his all-in move; for 2 reasons, 1 is that he thinks I have a weak hand and he wants to steal the pot and #2, if I call, he has the out of the straight, so it is a gamble he took and he won the bet. So, a bad beat but surely not the worst I ever have taken, and yes, I have put the bad beat on people also.

Yesterday's $300 buy in is the perfect example. It is like the 6th round and I have $30,000 in chips, I have an A/J, there is a no raise before the flop with 4 people in. The flop is J/8/6, and the first guy comes out going all-in and has more chips than I do. I know the guy and he plays a wild game and is capable of making any move. There was no raise before the flop, so I know he does not have an over pair. I think about how the whole hand played out and I put him on a move knowing he did not flop trips because he would not have gone all-in wanting someone to call. I call, the rest of the field folds.

Well, sometimes poker is like life and you think you have the answers only to find you were wrong, we turn over our hands and my mind is blown when he shows his pocket Qs; he outplayed me.

Now comes the good part of the story and a point of when you play a tournament, no matter how good you play you must get lucky in order to win. I cannot think of one poker tournament I have won that if I didn't get lucky even if it is just one time in one hand, I would not have won the tournament, this was one of those times. I am ready to call it a night and I stand up and drop my head as the turn card comes with a 7, the magical ace comes on the river.

I had over 60,000 in chips and I never looked back the rest of the night as cards seemed to run over me. The game went on another 6 hours and when all was said and done, I took the whole tournament down winning $4250 bucks and a free entry in the Tournament of Champions next Sunday worth $250. So, you just heard a good beat story, for me, not the guy who had QQ, but that ace on the river in actuality made me close to $4500. My chips stack when the game was over was 1,250,000 in chips.

And here is the poem I just wrote about that day.

"JUST ANOTHER DAY"

So today I got up early, it was around the crack of noon.

There was the Sunday tournament and it seemed to come too soon.

So, I hopped into to the shower and washed my new haircut do.

And I shaved my beard wanting people to say, "Is that you?"

I showed up 20 minutes late, but I still got right in

I had high hopes that this tournament I would win

And I got in a hand that I should have lost but to my demise

I put a bad beat on a guy and won the hand to my surprise

And I never looked back, and it seemed I could do no wrong

*I took first place in the tournament and now I sing my song.
I'm a winner, I'm a winner, and tonight I take home the chicken
dinner.*

CHAPTER 36

Halloween, October 31, 2019

I am going to stay home tonight so I can hand out candy to the Halloween kids.

It has always been one of my favorite days of the year. I have my mask ready, and I will do my traditional Trick or Treat. Being short helps me to try and fool one of my neighbors when I go their door and in a high-pitched voice I say, "Trick or Treat?" and in forty years of doing this I have yet to be busted.

This has been a good week in poker winning Sundays $300 buy in event and $4250 and a freeroll into the Tournament of Champions this next Sunday, and then I won $1250 coming in first place in Tuesday's $120. So close to a six grand week which gives me a nice feeling.

Funny how money plays such a big part of how we look at life. I mean I have never been a materialistic type of person so I have all that I need, I accept I will never have all that I want. Yet, I lack nothing really that I want or knowing that what I want could take away from what I have. Contentment is so much easier to have if you accept that what you have is all you need.

I am practicing my Father Ron costume I am wearing tomorrow to go to a costume party and how I will be preaching and blessing everyone and giving my bullshit advice when they come to me in confession. I do love Halloween.

Here is a poem I wrote 4/7/ 2016 when I was heading for Las Vegas.

"FANTASY LAND"

Roll the dice, flip the coin, fate decides where I am going

No real plans any real design, what is someone else's I want as mine

Call it greed; call it desire, looking for water when I am on fire

Just hop on a plane let fate set in

When in my fantasyland with a constant grin

I go all night it is later for sleep, consume all the garbage I will eat

And at the end of the trip, I will show my status, for everyday it is free gratis.

April 11, 2016, Las Vegas

Like an idiot trapped in paradise with my $100 in winnings so far in the four days I have been here. I mean I got in the money four out of five times in small tournaments putting me $1200 ahead. I won $600 in open play and being the retarded individual, I am put close to $2000 into the slot machines. I won back about half that amount but received 1500 award points putting me up to 6500 points for the year. I need 15,000 to keep my Diamond status which provides me free rooms, free food, and free show tickets.

I did the math in 2018 all tolled I lost $8000 for the year in slots to get my Diamond status. I stayed thirty-four nights in the year, went to ten shows, and received about $1200 in food. I got to be put on the top of the list when waiting for a seat for a poker game or to enter a restaurant. I love having a Diamond status. But I could have done the same thing paying for my rooms and food and shows for about half of what I lost playing slots.

As a gambler you lose your edge by playing slots knowing you cannot beat them in the long run, I wonder what fascination I get by playing them knowing the long-term outcome. But I think I love the sensations the slots provide, when you hit a big pay and just sit back as the bells and whistles go off. I never push the button for it to stop as I savor this time with pure joy. My neighbor next to me hates it as my tally keeps going up and he has lost his ass all night and has to listen to my winnings pile up. I know this feeling as I have been the neighbor of someone next to me is doing the same thing and I wonder about this lucky bastard as I am stuck listening to his music.

Valerie's two brothers and sister, Victor, Vincent and Vanessa, showed up with cousin Robin. They all live close to Vegas and we all went down to Freemont Street, it is an amazing place just to observe people, I love going there. I have decided to stay one more night as I am feeling lucky and have a pocket full of money. Valarie has to work in the morning, so she is leaving right after our trip to Freemont Street. I am getting second thoughts and think I should head home a $1200 winner for the four-day trip plus all the expenses. But no, I don't listen to myself.

April 12, 2016, still in Vegas

What a difference a day makes. I lost my ass. My feelings to leave the day before were right, but no I had a pocket full of money and wanted more, so I went to the players club and asked for my fifth free night. The agent got on his computer and saw my status and saw how much I had been playing the slots, they love slot players in Vegas it is how they keep building more casinos.

He replied, "Mr. Lemco not only we will extend you another day, but we will upgrade you to a suite!" And I checked into a room with a Jacuzzi, which I never used, including the room. I stayed up and played poker for twenty hours straight, I was down $2000 in a 3-5 no limit game and just couldn't quit.

The cards had turned against me. Four times on big pots I was ahead when I went all-in and four times I got beat on the river. I bought back in with my last $700 and finally got lucky; I mean my best handheld up and I won a $2000 pot against two other people all-in. I cashed out after twenty-one hours of play in time to make a flight heading back to Seattle in two hours. So up to my luxurious room I go, looking at the still- made bed and no time to even take a shower, just grabbed my bag and headed for the airport.

I counted my money as I sat in the taxi and I had $100 more then I left home with. I lost over $1100 the last night, but if I didn't win that last hand, I would have lost $2700 for the trip. So, I am thankful for the fun time I had, and I am looking forward to getting on the plane and get some sleep.

The real point of this story, I had lost control and if you want to be a professional poker player you must set limits. I should have known that when I got sucked out on the river the first time. I should have called it a night knowing the cards were not going my way and went and enjoyed my room, a Jacuzzi, got a good night's sleep and been close to $1200 ahead on the trip. So, I need to work on my control and learn not to get my nose open.

I wrote this next poem waiting to get on the plane.

"THE OUTCOME"

There were times I fell in crap, but I came out in cream

May have started as a nightmare but it ended in a dream

I studded down a burr covered road

But I kept on walking until the street turned into gold.

I have had some frights but very little fear

There were some concerns, but I never really cared

And yes, I been in the rain but I hardly got wet

Other people may worry but I seldom fret

May have lived in some places that were not my domain

I made the most of the environment because I was insane

There were times I wanted steak but hamburger I settled for

Happy with just getting by I never hungered to have more

If there was something I couldn't have, I just gave up the crave

I never found anything that was worth me becoming a slave.

CHAPTER 37

November 2, 2019

I am in one of my moods where I don't give a shit what I write about, I just feel like writing. I guess that is a good attribute for a writer, but when I am like this sometimes, I am not coherent as I am just out to please myself and not the reader.

What's Behind the Words is the name of my book and it is supposed to explain what inspired me to write a poem. This so-called book is now 167 pages and close to 53,000 words and ten years in the making, and I am not sure if any of it has made sense to the reader. And do I care? I really don't know.

I have been posting my everyday writing on Facebook and I get maybe five to ten people that respond. None of them say anything about what they think of the poem that brought about the chapter. Is it because my poems are not that good or did the reader just pass by the poem as I know poems are not for everyone?

Does it sound like I am complaining? No, I am just zooming along typing without too much thought and what you read is a flashing thought for me. Ok, enough of this, time to get serious, now that is funny as I don't take much seriously.

Stop it already Ron, write something with substance.

Oh, now you're telling me what to write, you don't have that kind of power over me.

I'm just saying that you're going in circles, I know better than to tell you what to do.

Ok I will just write a poem; they always make sense to me and sometimes bring me back to reality.

"SOMETIMES"

Sometimes things don't go just right,

When sleep is an issue, and you just toss and turn all night.

Sometimes you take a shower, and the water is cold

Sometimes you go to buy something, but it is already sold

Sometimes you fly stand-by and the flight is full

Sometimes the cards forget to follow the rules

Well, here are some answers when things don't go your way

Attitude is in charge from this you never sway

You have the power to turn the bad into good

You can't always do as you want but do as you should

See the up side to all your things that went wrong

Then you turn the blues into a song.

There I feel better now but I have lost the urge to write as my son Dane just texted me and invited me to come play some ping-pong and right now that sounds like more fun than writing. And I am sure when it comes to editing my book this chapter will not exist, unless for some reason I hear different from the readers that somehow this chapter had some entertainment value.

CHAPTER 38

November 3, 2019, 11 P.M.

I just home from the Muckleshoot and had another good day. It was the Tournament of Champions which happens once a month and I had won my entry into it last week along with $4500, and then Tuesday I took first place for $1200. And the tournament today we chopped four ways, each of us got $2160, and Eric who was chip leader by a mile took first place for $4000.

The point is I really don't have the right to brag about my poker playing but I do brag about being the way I am, I am totally happy with myself. I like that I am mellow, and I don't let shit get to me. That I give whenever I can, when I see the need only because what you give you get back. I so believe that. I not going to tell the ways I give, but I give often, not only money but care and concern about others, it just comes natural to me, I want to.

Does it sound like I am bragging or like I am some kind of Saint or something that sure is not my point, I am advising all my friends to feel and be the same way because I know of the rewards you receive being the way I am. That's silly; I know everyone is what they are, but just try to sink in what I am trying to say. And I am not sure what I am trying to say.

Two points I guess that you can add to your personality without having to change yourself.

#1. Attitude is a choice, you get to choose how you will take things, even when bad happens search for the good with-in, if it is a learning experience, then it wasn't all that bad.

When good happens, you will savor it even more. Don't let others bring you down, that happens so often, you control only yourself, and others can't if you don't let them.

#2. Give and give again, not only money but with understanding, with forgiveness, you will find it comes back in the shape of luck and happiness.

My God, what is happening to me, I dress up as Father Ron to go to a Halloween party and all of a sudden, I am preaching to the world. Sorry folks, I am just feeling my oats right now and I am so content, that I want all my friends and family to feel the same joy.

I guess I will always be a dreamer.

"I CAN'T CLIMB A MOUNTAIN"

All the past days where they ever went

I look forward to the tomorrows as I walk by slow

The legs are not close to what they used to be

My health is the price I pay for being me

I have done and been what I want whenever I choose

I seem to have got away with it, for now I have nothing to lose

Now I can't climb a mountain, it's no big deal

When I always got away with doing whatever I feel

Eating shit and smoking and play poker all night

I always felt exercise were for those who want to fight

I always choose down-hill paths they are easier to walk

And why do physical work if you know how to talk

Why drink water when there is Fireball and Diet Coke

I find all the talk about health foods as kind of a joke

Sure, I am 72 years old and mountains I can't climb

And I wonder if I have left very much behind

If asked by my kids or even a really good friend

If I had it all to do over, I would do the same again

What's Behind the Words?

CHAPTER 39

November 5, 2019

Yesterday was a turnaround of my luck at the Muckleshoot tournament. Everything that could go wrong did, I played well, but my very firsthand I had A/J and the flop is A/J/4. I check and the guy mini bets. I just call and the turn card comes another 4. I bet two times the pot bet and the guy raise double my bet, I now don't like the 4 and I just call.

The river is an air-ball and I check with top two pairs and the guy makes a big bet, which was over half my stack, I got to call. He did not have a 4, he had two of them, and he had quad 4s. He said I wish I knew you were so strong I would have bet more, and he is right I probably would have called, but he wanted to bait me and not lose me.

I still had half my chips. I came back and made it three more hours until there were sixteen players left and I was short stack and made a move with K/J and ran into pocket 10s. Oh well.

I head to the 1/3 spread game and my buddy Johnny the Jew (that's what I call him) is in the game and I buy in for $300. About the third hand I play I have A/K, two guys call $3 bucks and Johnny raises to $20 bucks, and the two other people call. I know Johnny plays aggressive and I make a move to win the $70 bucks in the pot and I come out making it $100 in hopes everyone folds. I hate A/K, it is the most overrated hand, more money is lost with A/K than any other hand, and I usually just call with the hand after a raise. If your ace or king flops no one puts you on the hand and you get paid, if nothing comes, you can get out of the hand cheap. Everyone folds accept Johnny who goes all in for $170, well I am priced in and the pot odds make me call, but I know I am behind now and putting Johnny on a nice pair, but it is a shootout. I thought so until he turned over his pocket Ks and no ace comes, and Johnny takes down the $400 pot. I have about $60 left which I blow off next hand playing an 8/9 of diamonds and the flop is a 6/7, but I don't hit after pushing all my chips in and I head home $420 down. That folks are poker; you take the good with the bad and after winning $8000 last week I will just accept it.

It makes me think of when I was an Uber driver and I picked up a guy with no legs and the attitude he had about life always up-lifts me. I guess I will close today's writing with the ride in hopes it makes you the reader see how lucky you are, sometimes without even knowing it.

October 12th, 2015

Stayed out until 3:30 am doing Uber, did well, picked up another story for my book. Yep, all falling into place, hope to publish by years end.

Here is the second story in, the chapter, "Riders Who Inspire."

I received a call to go about three miles from where I was at, since I was in downtown Seattle, I found the ride out of the ordinary for Uber works this system, the driver that is the closes to the call receives the ride, I was sure there were drivers closer than I was, and almost rejected the call, as I knew within a minute or so I would receive a call within blocks of where I was at. But I took it and it goes to show that many things that happen in life have a reasoning behind them, if you care to look.

When I got to the location there was man in a wheelchair waiting for me. He had no legs; I felt a little awkward in not knowing how to handle this situation. Normally I stop and the passenger hops right in, do I jump out and help this man get in, do I fold up his wheelchair and put it in the trunk? Do I need to lift him into the car? All these questions were answered as my back door came open the man with one movement of his arms lifted himself into the back seat, then reaching out in one quick movement, he pushed a button on his chair, and it folded up, he then lifted it into the back seat.

                          What's Behind the Words?

"Thanks for picking me up, and how are you doing today?" I was bewildered by the ease the man had been, so self- efficient and I simply replied, "I am doing ok, how about you?" What he said next changed the way I greeted passengers from that day forward, it was such a natural reply, and it hit me like a ton of bricks.

"Ronald, attitude is a choice, and my choice is to always be happy, so I guess I am just fine, thanks for asking!"

All riders receive the name of the driver who is coming to get them, but I appreciated the fact he used mine, but his answer was so magnificent, especially from a man with no legs. It was like he read my mind when I had my dumbfounded look, but it really was a look of admiration.

"You're wondering why I have my kind of attitude when I have no legs?"

"No," I stuttered by him reading my mind, and not wanting to admit it but decided right then that I liked this guy, and I was going to be up front with him. "Well, yeah, I was kind of wondering, but I didn't have the balls to say so. How do you do it?"

"It is like I said about attitude, I have no legs there is nothing I can do about it, and therefore I make the most of what I do have." I loved his reply and listened as he talked when he said something I had said for years, all my kids grew up with me preaching it, and now I was about to hear it from someone else.

He was telling me about his third tour to Iraq when he had stepped on a land mind losing his legs. He had woken up in the hospital three days later, first time knowing of the loss of his legs. His first reply was "Bummer". WTF, I thought, your first reply about losing your legs was bummer. Bummer, like when you drop the milk carton, when you stub your toe, when the dog sits on the carpet, that was what I thought was a bummer.

He went on telling me the most optimistic things about life and how he savored all the good. He said when you can deal with the bad and see good within it, well it makes you enjoy the good when it come all the more.

My saying to the kids was "The winners in life are those who deal with the bad the best", so when the good comes you savor it even more than it is. When you can take the bad and find something good within, even if it was just a lesson, then the bad wasn't so bad after all. To hear almost the same words from this legless man was really inspiring. He was married and had two children, He was going to shoot pool leaving in the evening and not wanting to bother his wife decided to Uber. He said he was going to be doing some drinking or he would have taken his car that had all hand controls.

The more this man talked the more inspiration I had for him; he had a job working for a big Tech Company in Redmond. He never saw himself as being handicapped.

I dropped him off at a tavern where he slid his wheelchair out, opened it up, pulled himself onto it and rolled away. I wondered how he would shoot pool without legs, but after talking to this man, I knew he could accomplish anything he wanted to do, to me this man is a hero.

And when you think the world is against you, think of this man, his attitude which he chooses is by far a most remarkable attribute. And there is a lesson for life "ATTITUDE IS A CHOICE"

"YESTERDAY, TODAY AND TOMORROW"

Yesterday seems so long ago when I was just a boy

Yet it only seems like yesterday that I remember the joy

The time went by quick, but memories are here to stay

But what good does it do to reminisce, what's important is today

Today is real; it's the now, the reality of it all

It doesn't really matter all that you did before

Today I have the bad, the hate, and all of the fear

But I also have the good, my loving God and my lady dear

Yes, today comes with the good but also there is the sorrow

But all the feelings they might change come tomorrow

Tomorrow is on the way; it is closer than it may seem

*It could furnish you with unhappiness' or could give you
your dream*

It could deliver you to the kingdom or to the devil's domain

Just depends on the life you live and the one you claim

Yes, yesterday, today, and tomorrow we will see all three

Only thing I know for sure is this life I lived was free.

CHAPTER 40

November 15, 2019

It is funny that when I just typed today's date, I remembered it was my second son Devin's birthday, and I am always shocked to remember how old my kids are getting. Devin is 36 years old today; my fat little funny baby is a middle-aged man. I just called him to wish him Happy Birthday but got his answering machine, which speaks to how the world is today. Everyone has a life and is busy and there is so much, yet they have to do and time for little idiocies is put on the back burner.

I have not written any in my book for ten days as I to have so much to do, not have to do, but want to do. And when I hoped to finish by this year's end has become a pipe dream as my book comes in second place to the things I want to do.

Like the last five days I spend in Las Vegas, that was something I wanted to do, and it turned out great as I came home with as much money as I left with having a fantastic time.

I got to spend time with old friends, I got to hug and kiss Stacy, who beat cancer and is such an inspiration to me. I got to be with and old friend and business partner Don Ganson.

I got in the money four out of six tournaments I played, and believe it or not, I actually came out ahead playing slot machines. Stupid that I even play them, but because I do, I have Diamond status which gets me free rooms, food show tickets and getting in front of all lines.

Ever since I decided this is really a book about my life, I am not afraid to show my faults, for they are part of me and my life.

Now I will grab one of my journals and tell you about what I was going through at that portion of my life.

June 14, 2016

I am of on my last hurrah with $5000 to blow at the World Series of Poker, but with hopes it doesn't come to that. I will play two senior events at $1000 each; I will play some $300 satellites to win an entry in the Main Event. I have five days booked at the Rio which was all I could get for free; if I am doing well, I will pay for any further days, but at discount prices. I am very excited and going down with confidence & focus.

I drove a lot of Uber this week and got a few good stories for my next book "Uberman" plus I made close to $1000.

I think about my lifestyle and think of a Joe Walsh verse in one of his songs, "People say I am lazy, but it takes all my time." Or another Eagle song, "I am a Joker, I am a smoker, I am a midnight toker, but I just want to have a good time." I am living a dream in what I feel are my final years, and if you want to know how I feel, I would say. "I am totally content"

To win a bracelet is my ultimate bucket list desire.

I really wonder how long I have left living the lifestyle I have chosen. Oh well, every day is like a free gratis day for me and I will savor it knowing as Frank Sinatra sang. "I did it my way".

I have lived a blessed life and never want anyone to feel sad for me.

I am the Motengator Kid.

"A QUICKY"

Getting older just don't seem right

As I take my teeth out at night

I look in the mirror and ponder

Or maybe it is more of a wonder

Is the reflection that I, see?

Is that the real inner me?

Na, its ingrown kid inside

That has kept this old body alive

For I choose no kind of fear

Or have what some would consider a scare
So once again I say with rejoice
Attitude is totally your choice

What's Behind the Words?

CHAPTER 41

November 16, 2019, 11:30 P.M.

What a kick back day it was, I stayed in bed until 5pm, think I had some catching up to do from my Vegas trip.

Thanksgiving is closing in I find it one of the best holidays of the year, I think they should change the name to Thanks forgiving which has two meanings, one would be a thank you for all you gave during the year, you know when you give of the heart without expecting any return, you just want to give. To a charitable organization, a homeless person you see on the street. Time to someone in need of a friend, there are so many ways a person can give and for those times I say Thanks for giving. The second thanks come with the word forgiving. I think it is a great time of the year to forgive, to let go of a grudge, a political argument. For a fellow member of the family who you, for some reason don't see eye to eye with, one who sees things different than you. I say so what, we are family if you cannot forgive your blood, then I feel I failed in raising you. There is nothing more important to me in my life then my family and us all being family is the best thing anyone could do for me.

Tonight, I called my oldest friend Jim Bartlett to invite him and his beautiful wife Donita over for an early Thanksgiving dinner next Saturday. For fifty years we have been friends, but it seemed to fade away with our differences about politics, I mean total difference. We fought on the internet, so hard and calling each other names, that we blocked each other. Now that is when it gets stupid to let our opinions get in the way of a fifty-year friendship. There is no way I was going to change his opinion, nor he change mine. So, I guess we just do not talk politics and accept to agree to disagree.

And there is a third Thanks that deserves recognition. Thanks to God. I am not going to preach to you about any certain God, but I believe he exists, I know for me personally that I am truly blessed and have the life I live, the things I have because of that blessing, I wake everyday thanking my God for just another day. I thank him for all the things most of us take for granted, things you forget you are blessed with but if you lacked you would understand the blessing. And then there is all you do have which deserves a Thank-You.

Alright Ron, enough of the preaching, don't you have a book to write?

Yeah, sometimes I just go off, but I truly hope that there are messages that help others in my writings.

April 2008

I hate smoking, it is easy to quit I have done it hundreds of times. Every time I light a smoke I feel like a loser. How do I let it control me, but it does? I know all the harms it is causing, but the urge grabs me and kicks my minds ass and I light up another cigarette.

There is a new drug out to help you stop smoking called Chantix, it advertises to take away the urge, you continue to smoke the first two weeks after you start taking the medicine and the urge to smoke slowly disappears. It is expensive but I am willing to try it. Son of a gun after two weeks the urge to smoke is gone. I no longer think about lighting up, this is magical. This stuff really works.

I do have some really weird dreams, some I enjoyed that were sexual, I do feel a little irritated, but I am thinking it is due to the lack of nicotine. I woke up at 4am in my third week of taking Chantix and reached for my bottle of sleeping pills, I took the whole bottle and went back to sleep not even knowing what I did.

This is crazy but my dog Dylan is barking and scraping my door, it is like he knows I am in danger. My Brother-in-law Victor is staying with us and goes to see what the commotion is. He knocks on my door but when I don't answer, he opens my door and sees the color I am and knows something is wrong. He calls 911 and they show up in time to take me to the hospital and have my stomach pumped, my life was saved, thanks Dylan and Victor.

The hospital says I have mental issues and suicidal thoughts and sent me to some sort of mental institution called Fairfax north of Seattle.

I wrote this poem after a few days there.

"FAIRFAX HIGH"

The law says I need to check into this place

It is called Fairfax high where they look for a trace

Of what it was that got me here,

Was it paranoia, suicidal, or just plain old fear?

They have these doctors that have seen and heard it all

They listen to your story then they make the call

With their experience and with all they have seen

They know if you belong here or there or in-between

They prescribe you drugs to bring you out of harm

And bring you back to where you feel you are charmed

They draw you a map for you to escape

To the downside you're at to better gate

And clues get easier, and visions become real

The doctors think they know how I should feel

It was in you all along the doctors just remove the shell,

Now you have the vision of heaven, you are now rejecting hell.

I am in group counseling right now as Valarie is waiting for a visit with me, she brought me a bag of stuff, it would be nice to have a conjugal visit, but I know it is a pipe dream. After the group meeting me and Val have lunch together.

"Honey, what were you thinking" she asks.

"I wasn't thinking, I had no idea what I was doing."

I can tell Valarie is worried about me, but she has been married to me long enough to wonder if I have something up my sleeve. This time it was nothing I planned as in the past when I pulled off employment injuries and got some good settlements. Yet this episode turns out to bring about the best pay day of them all, and I wasn't even trying.

I spend seven days at Fairfax, and I made the most of the time along with sound advice from some of the doctors. If I would have known that the lawsuit against Chantix which would take 4 years would have got me $175,000 or $25,000 a day, shit I would have stayed a month. Yeah, my lawyer buddy Mitch Zager hears the story and says let's sue.

It turns out when Chantix first came out, they did not have any warnings about the side effects of taking the pill. And it appears like there had been a few suicides and many attempts. Chantix settles in a joint action suit for millions of dollars, of which I got clear $95,000 after all the lawyer and other fees.

Yes, life is full of surprises and hidden blessings even for those who may not deserve it. But who am I to question fate?

"NEED TO BOAST"

The questions and the answers come in separate stages

And there is a hidden agenda that keep within me that rages

And you seek so hard when it is better to coast

When you try to be humble, but you need to boast

You try to be quick, but your inner wants to shout

You try to listen to the doctors who know that they are talking about.

And acceptance is the answer it is what it takes to make you free

---

CHAPTER 42

November 21, 2019, 6:06 P.M.

Well, I have few minutes to kill before I head off to the Muckleshoot Casino and play the Thursday night poker tournament that starts at 7:15. I been running sour lately, last night for example I played a really tight game. I played one hand in the first hour and I won it which got me back to my original 13,000 in chips. There were no more re-entrees so again I just waited for a hand. And finally, I got KK on the button. It was a 1600 blind and four players smooth called, so I thought of all the times I got sucked out on by slow playing and there was already almost 7,000 in the pot, I went all in with about 10,500 I had left, I did not care if anyone called, but one caller would be nice which would more than double me up. I got my wish as all, but one player folded and the caller called me with 55, I love it, right. Well, the flop is three diamonds, he has the 5 of D, I have no diamonds and sure enough without the wait the fourth Diamond hits and I go home early.

And that is called poker, I am a six- to-one favorite, but sometimes the odds make no difference. You just say nice hand.

I have learned that when luck is not with you, don't push it. I could have gone and played the live game, but I have learned take a bad beat as a sign, call it a night and go back tomorrow.

I have been thinking about my time working and driving for Uber and Lyft and I miss it, I really enjoyed the two years I did that. I decided to quit after my third accident along with the fact that my eyes were not as good as they used to be. After the accidents and the many close calls, I could let myself be in harm's way but not the other people I was responsible for. You need to know when to call it quits. Besides, I accomplished my goal of having enough material to write my Uberman book.

Tonight, I drove in Pierce County which pays the least out of all the counties I drive in. Pierce County only pays me $1 per mile and12 cents a minute, compared to the normal $1.35 and 25 cents a minute.

I just got home, and it is Saturday night, and it is only midnight. Saturday is usually the best and most profitable night to drive. I drove 140 miles and worked six hours and only made $77, way short of my normal. But it was one of those nights when the calls were miles away and they were only going short distances along with the fact I was in Pierce County.

Like I have said there are the good things within the bad, if you have the will to find them. My second to the last ride were four young men just over twenty-one who wanted to go to a local pub I am familiar with called the Log Cabin, located close to my house. I have taken many riders there. I like the place because they have a ping-pong table there and ping- pong is my road game which I have always excelled at. I had years of practice always having a ping-pong table growing up and a dad that loved to play. Combine that with the four years I played some pretty good players while I served my time in prison, well I played a mean game.

There was kid in the back seat talking smack how he was the best ping-pong player that ever lived, and how his buddies did not have a chance against him. He just kept on bragging.

I thought of Paul Newman in "Cool Hand Luke, I can eat 50 eggs" and the kid was starting to bug me with his bragging. I just could not contain myself.

"Tell you, young man, I may be an old man, but I will play you for fifty bucks to a game of 21."

"You got a deal old man" he cracked back at me and laughed out loud saying under his breath. "This will be the easiest fifty bucks I ever made; you don't know what you got yourself into."

The kid did have a good game, but he lost to me 18 to 21. He took the loss like a man and handed me $50. I took $20 and handed him back $30 telling him to buy a round of drinks for his friends, who were really ragging on him the whole game and rooting for me.

As I walked out, I said out loud. "Don't underestimate an old man and remember the roads you take; well, that old man made the trail.

I had gone offline when I walked into the Tavern and as soon as I got back in the car and went back on line, I got a Lyft call for a ride. The ride was 8 miles away and I thought about canceling the call as and end a discouraging night, other than winning the ping-pong game. I decided to take the call as it was the only Lyft ride for the night and Lyft pays the same no matter where you drive. I drove the eight miles to the Red Robin gourmet burger place and picked up a young couple who were only going a half mile away to the Best Western Hotel and I thought I should have gone with my first feelings and gone home.

They had just got married; I said congratulations and told them that I have been married thirty-four years. It only took a few minutes to get them to their destination. As I pulled up to the hotel the wife asked what was the secret for a lasting marriage. I almost told them that it was my fifth marriage that life is a game of numbers and eventually you hit a winner, but I didn't. I decided to tell them what ingredients Valarie and I had in order to make a marriage last.

"The key ingredient to a lasting marriage is Friendship, that no one is perfect, and friends can overcome the others short comings, that friends accept each other as they are and do not try to change them. The reason you guys got married is you like each other, like is sometimes more important than love. If you change your partner, you could lose what you fell in love with, so Friendship is the secret to a lasting marriage."

They both replied that each other were best friends and I said as they climbed out of the car, "Good never lose your friendship and you guys will last."

So ended my night as I started the eight miles back to my house thinking that maybe I helped a young couple with a few simple words that were the truth for me.

                    What's Behind the Words?

"OLD MAN"

The knowledge of time locked up in his head

People look and think, what's he doing out of bed

His face is wrinkled, his eyes show age

His hair has seen the different shades of greys

His mind strong and able to teach

To show the pit how to become a peach

The look of antiquity scares fellow creatures away

But with all his acquirements, he has much to say

He tries to be heard but to no avail

The roads you take, he made the trail.

CHAPTER 43

November 24, 2019

I have declaimer and that is I am in control of my book and I can do with it anything I want. I have no clear vision on how I am going to end this book. I mean it was supposed to be about my life and the poems I have written. But I have over a thousand poems and I have used only fifty in this book.

I've had five marriages, I've had three years in the carnival, I've spent four years in prison for robbing a bank, I've had six children, I've tried numerous businesses, fifty years of playing poker and still way ahead and if I wasn't me, I would wonder how much of this book is fiction.

The old saying that truth is stranger than fiction applies to my life story and for all the strangeness' one might see about my life, I only see it as all that was meant to be. I don't how I could or if I would want to change the way my life turned out. Maybe some things along the way if I could go back, but we know we cannot go back, so there is acceptance to how I was in order to be who I am.

I guess this is the long way to say I have decided to end this first half of my book.

Yes, I said half, after almost two-hundred pages and 63,000 words in the first half it would make continuing turn the book into an epic and I do not qualify to be in that category.

Maybe it is my incautiousness that I don't feel pressured by anyone to keep going. Who knows, maybe I am bored with how my book is turning out and the only way to find out how good this book is to judge it by those who read the first half and who want me to continue to the second half.

It could be that few people will like at all. I mean after all who cares about another person's life, especially someone who has no idea who you are. And for the five hundred people who I do know, who are friends with me on Facebook, well you got to follow along with my book as I posted each of my chapters as I finished them. So why buy a cow if you already got milk.

Really, there is much more work for me to do as now the editing comes into the play, and editing means, edit then edit again and when you're done doing that it is time to edit once more, then when it is ready to submit to the publisher and you read the transcript one more time and you still see mistakes, it is never ending.

So, I would say by years end there will be copies available for anyone interested.

There is so much more to my story along with some secrets I have kept to myself and was about to divulge, but hey, I got to have something to bring you back.

I want to thank all the people who have followed me and for the input I received from you that helped me to keep going and also make some changes.

I'm lying I did not need any encouragement to do my book, it was a lifetime in the making and I loved doing it, I loved seeing the replay of my life, all the reminiscing I got to do because I wrote this book. As I did, I wondered how lucky I was to be born in America as any other country may have assassinated me.

In actuality "What's Behind the Words" was the first book I was writing which I started fifteen years ago but something in life brought changes and I did my first two novels Rest Stop and Women in Circumstance and the book Uberman before I got around to finishing this book, which turns out to only being half done.

I know that life has never quit amazing me that no matter what was going on it was far from a boring life, I am not special, but I feel my life like everybody's unique, and beyond any doubt I am what I am because of experience. Not what experience did to me but what I did with the experience?

Well, since this is also a book of poems, I will write a brand-new poem to end this book.

In the meantime, my friends always remember "Attitude is a Choice". You get to choose how you want to see life, take the good and the bad, there is no avoiding either, but your attitude is in your full control.

"A LIFETIME"

Well, I will be damned that I would use the words Fickle
Finger of Fate

How can you start a poem off that way if you want it
to be great?

But there must be an explanation how my life all came to be

I would have to say that fate had a big part in the
making of me.

For I never was a planner many times acting before I gave
much thought

It was when I was in a fickle and surrounded it was then
that I fought

I seem to come together when pressure seemed too just
close on in

It was then when I pulled it all together it was then I
would begin

And through a life of trial and tribulations of coming out
on the top

When it all seemed kind of hopeless, but I did not know
the word stop

I was at my best when things were not just falling into place

When all seemed hopeless it was then that fate would
show a trace

I would be led to some kind of a horizon just a touch
out of sight

*But fate always seemed to have a way to make it all come
out alright.*

*Sure, I traveled many roads even when many came to
a dead end*

*And fate would show itself once again that it really
was my friend*

And I should not leave out God and my thanks that he is great

*For God was the inventor of the notorious Fickle
Finger of Fate.*

Ron and Steve Lemco in 1996
"Two Brothers take 1st and 2nd in poker tournament"

Ron's family in 2012
Drew, Ron, Valarie, Devin, Destiny and Dane

Ron, Valarie, and Destiny Lemco WSU Graduation 2017

Ron and Valarie's Engagement Photo - 1982